Mandala Coloring Book

EG PUBLISHING

A GIFT FROM

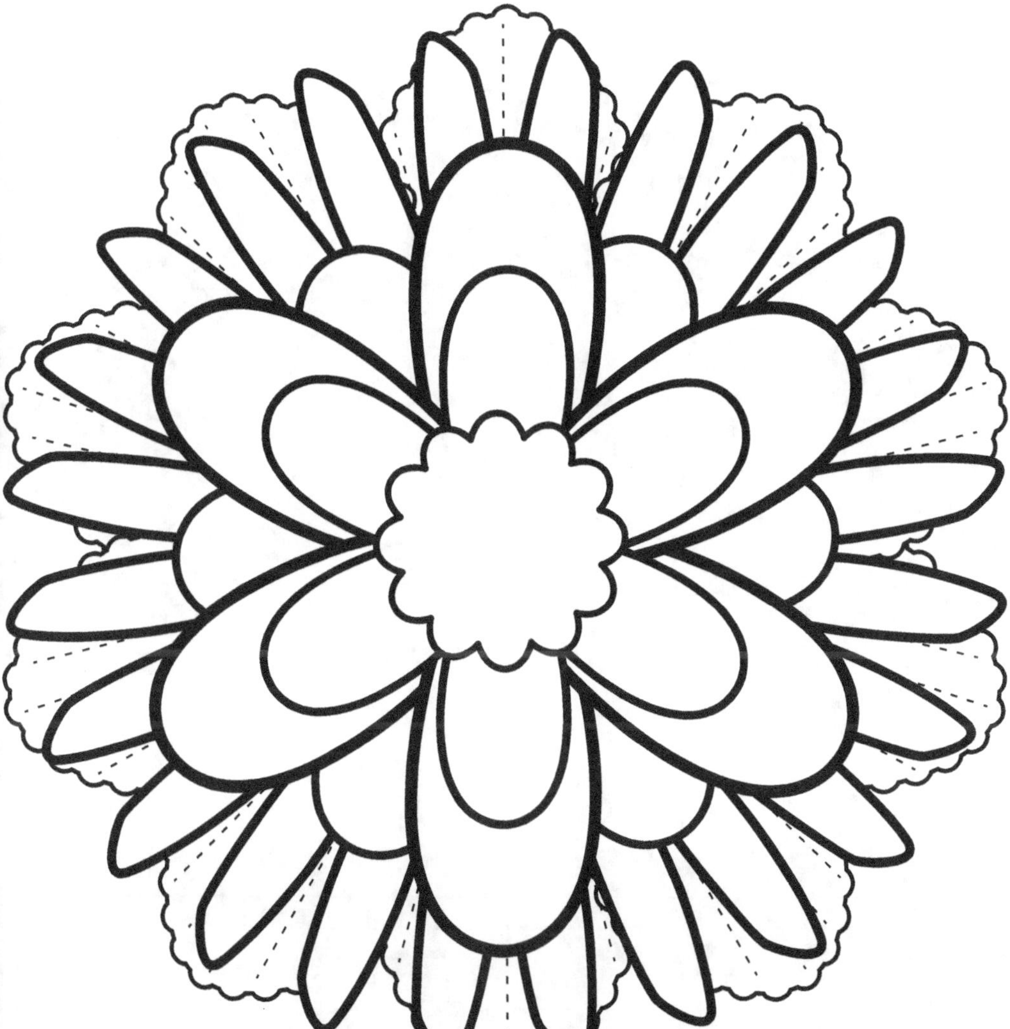

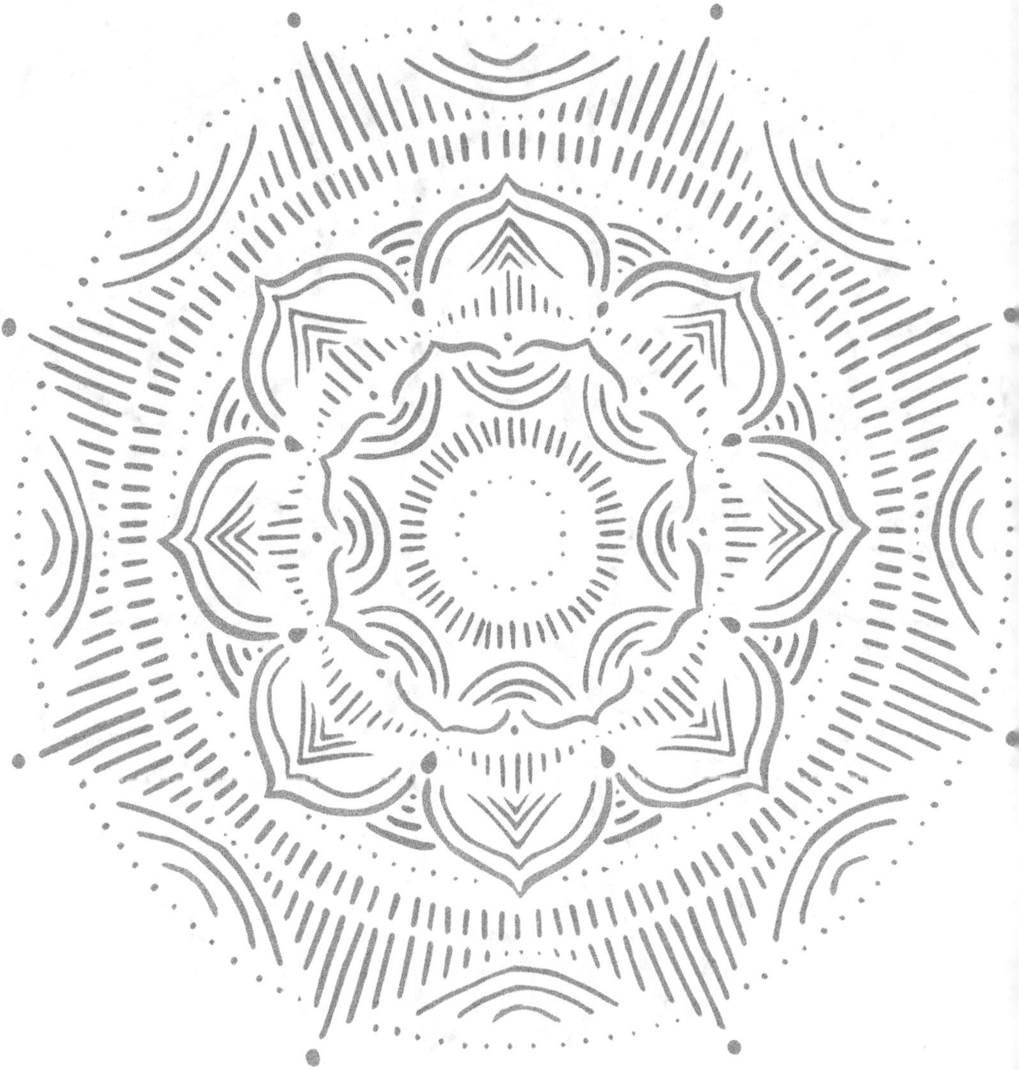

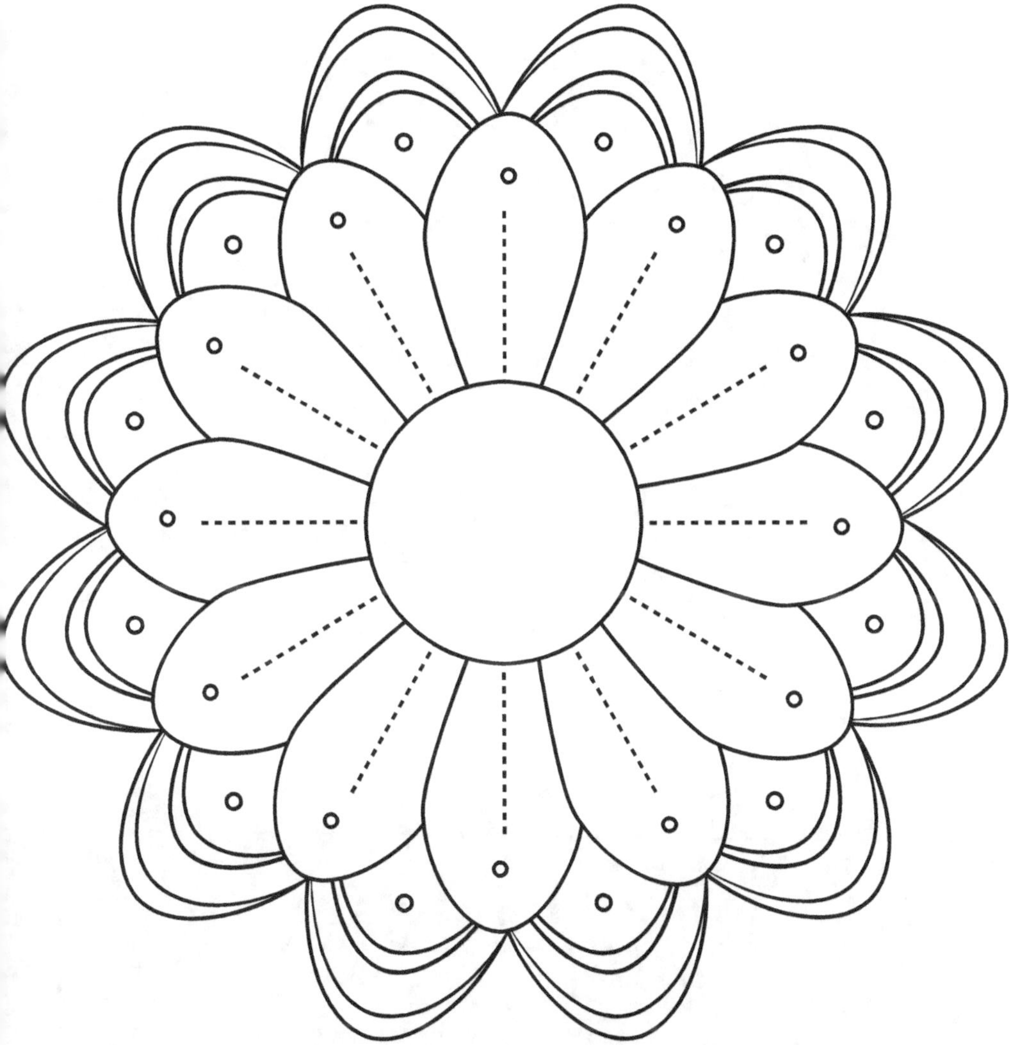

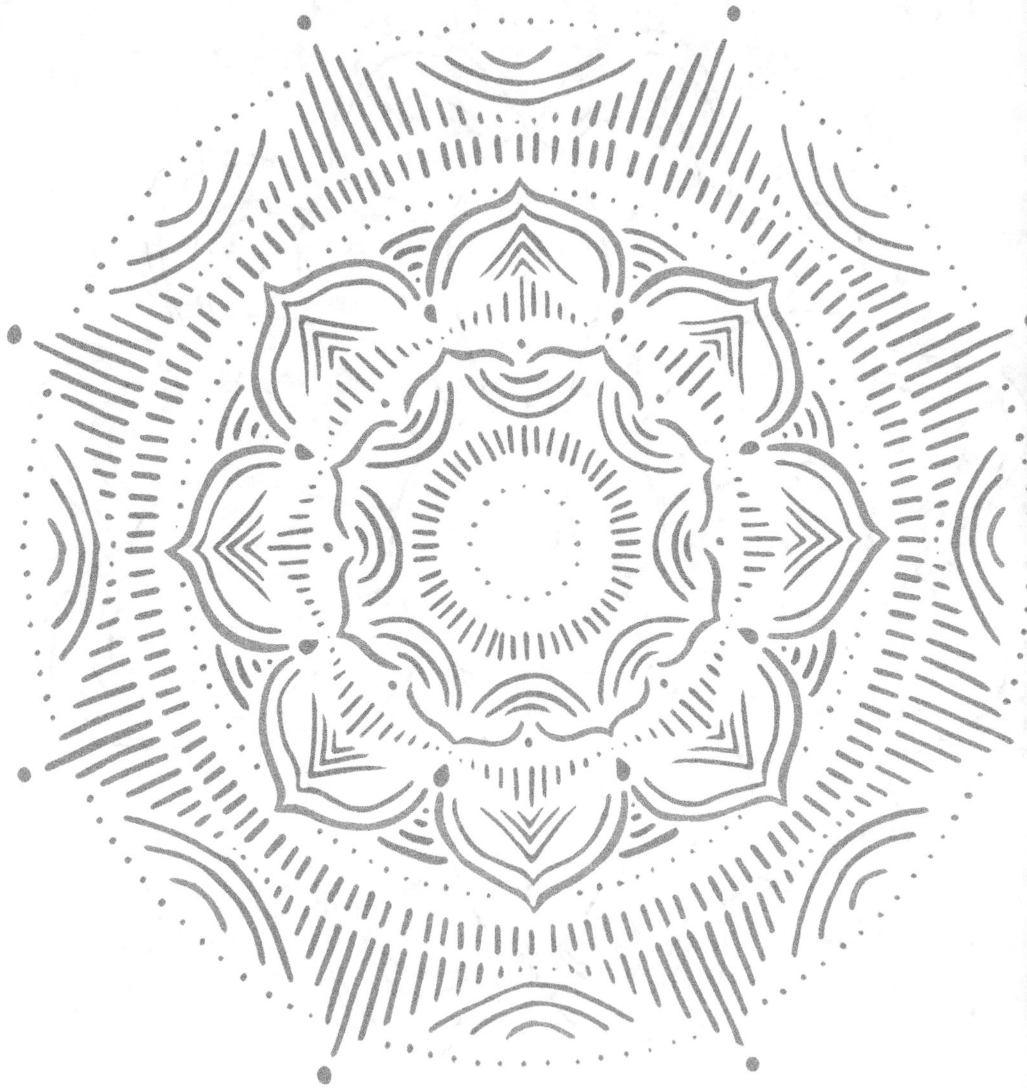

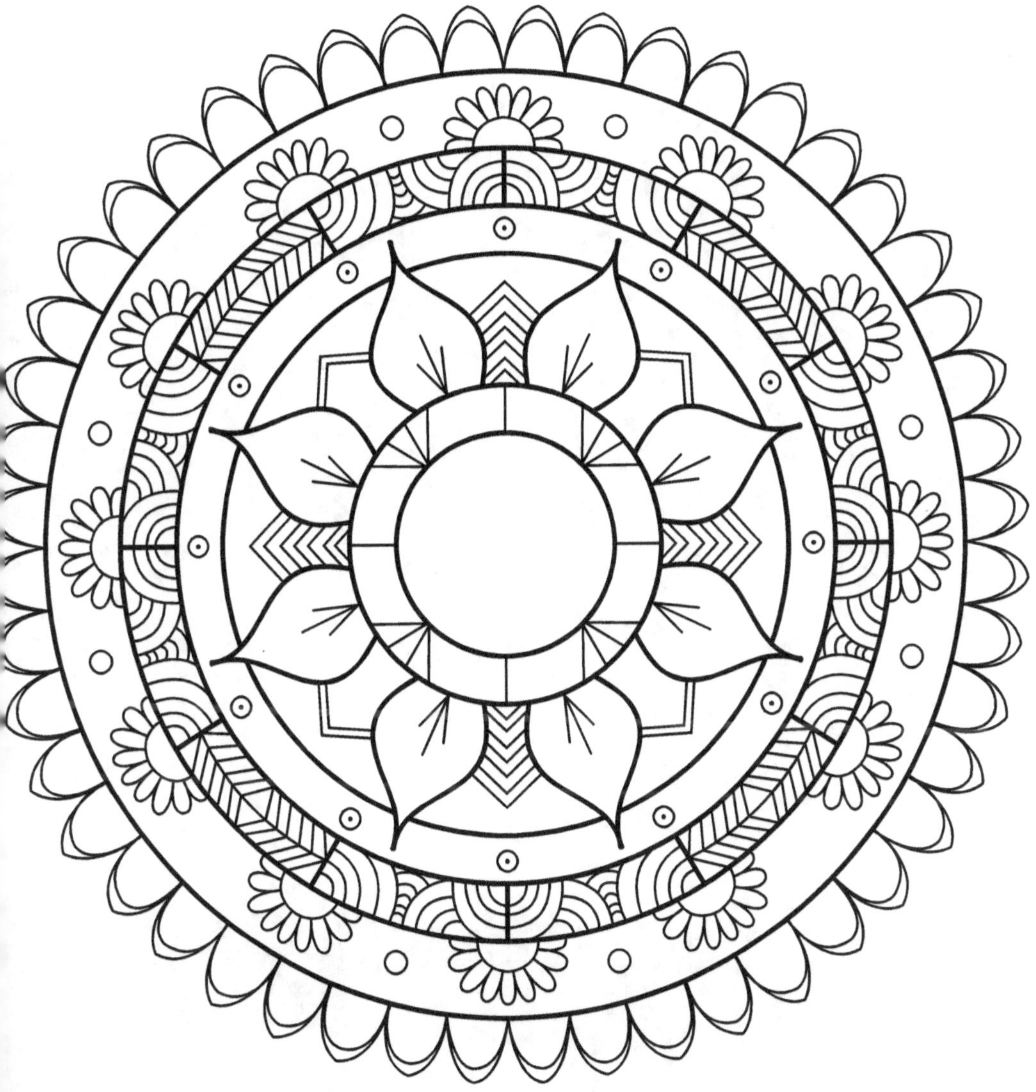

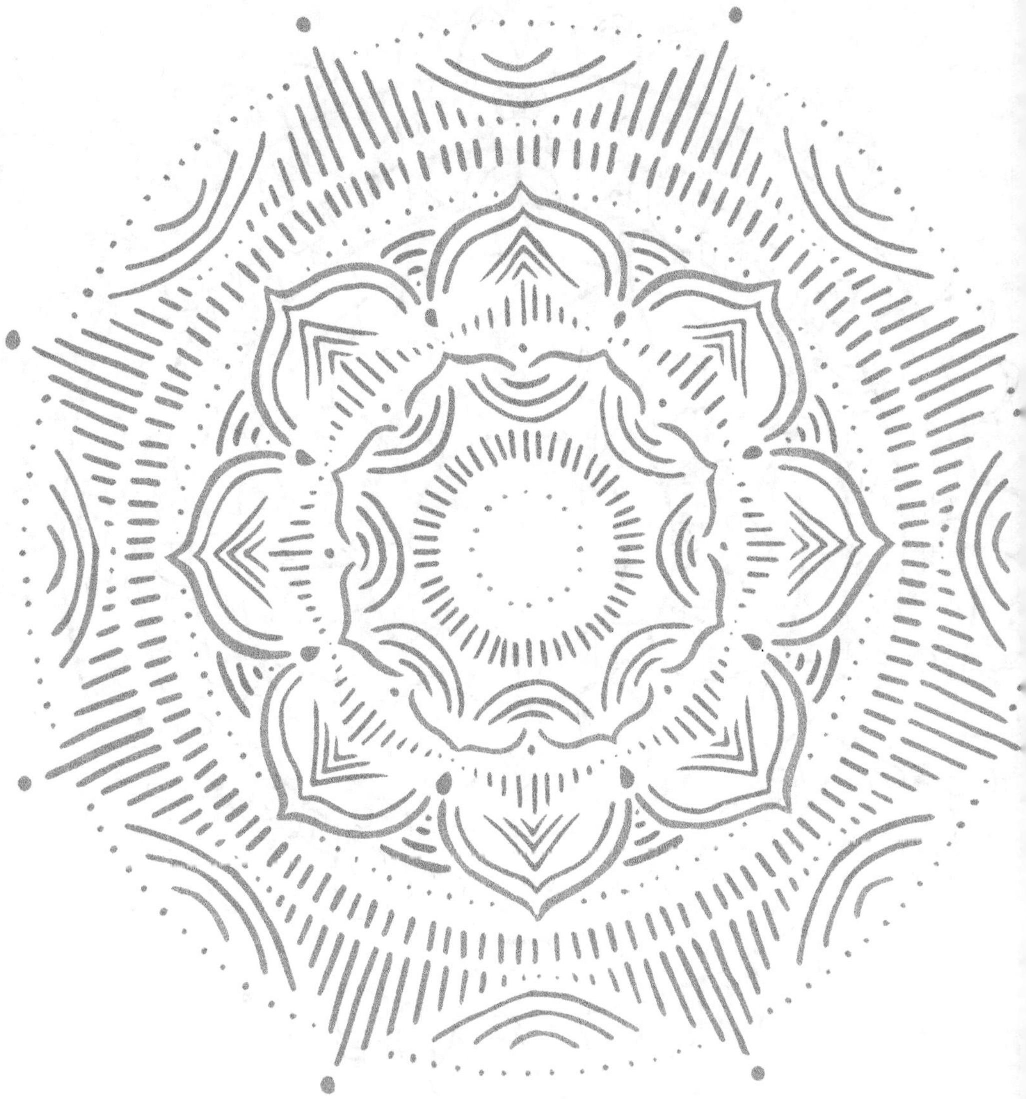

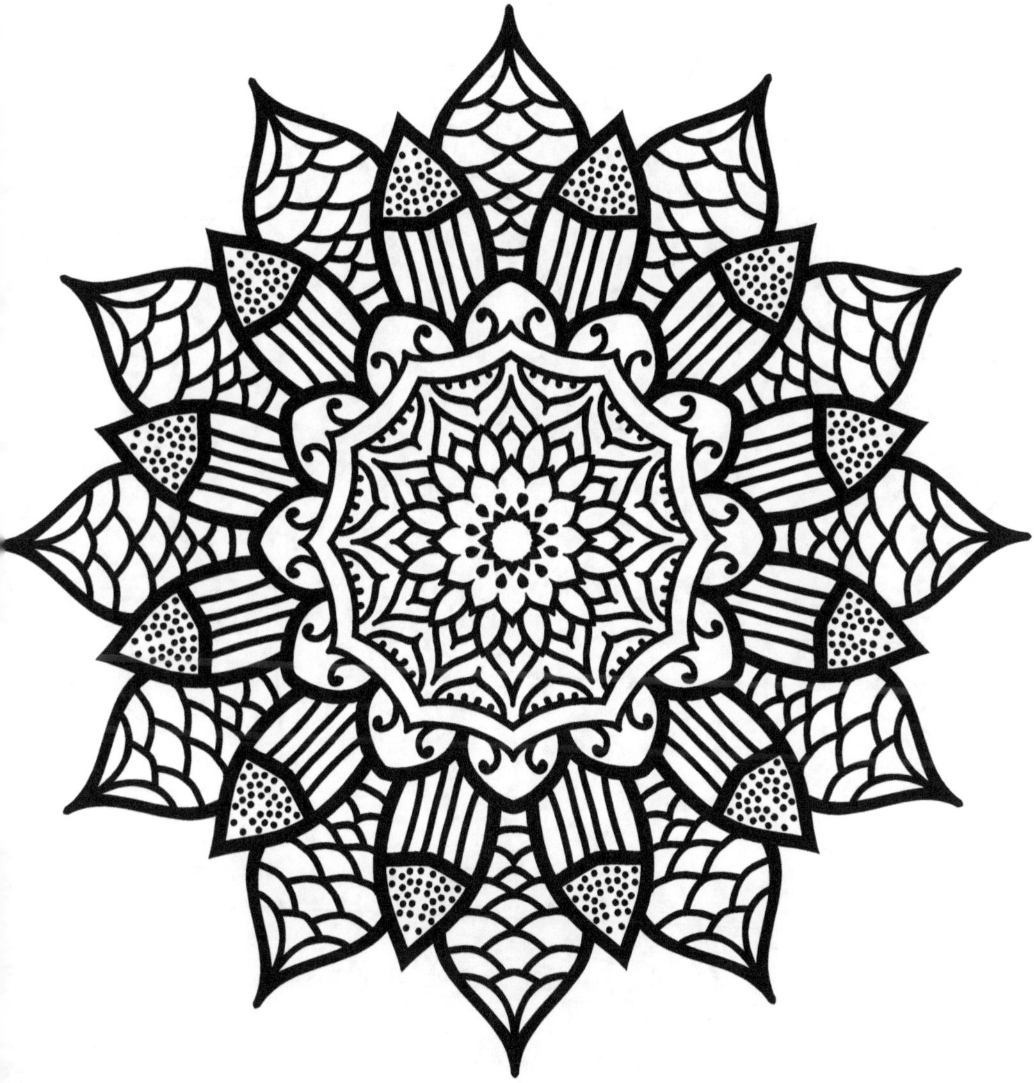

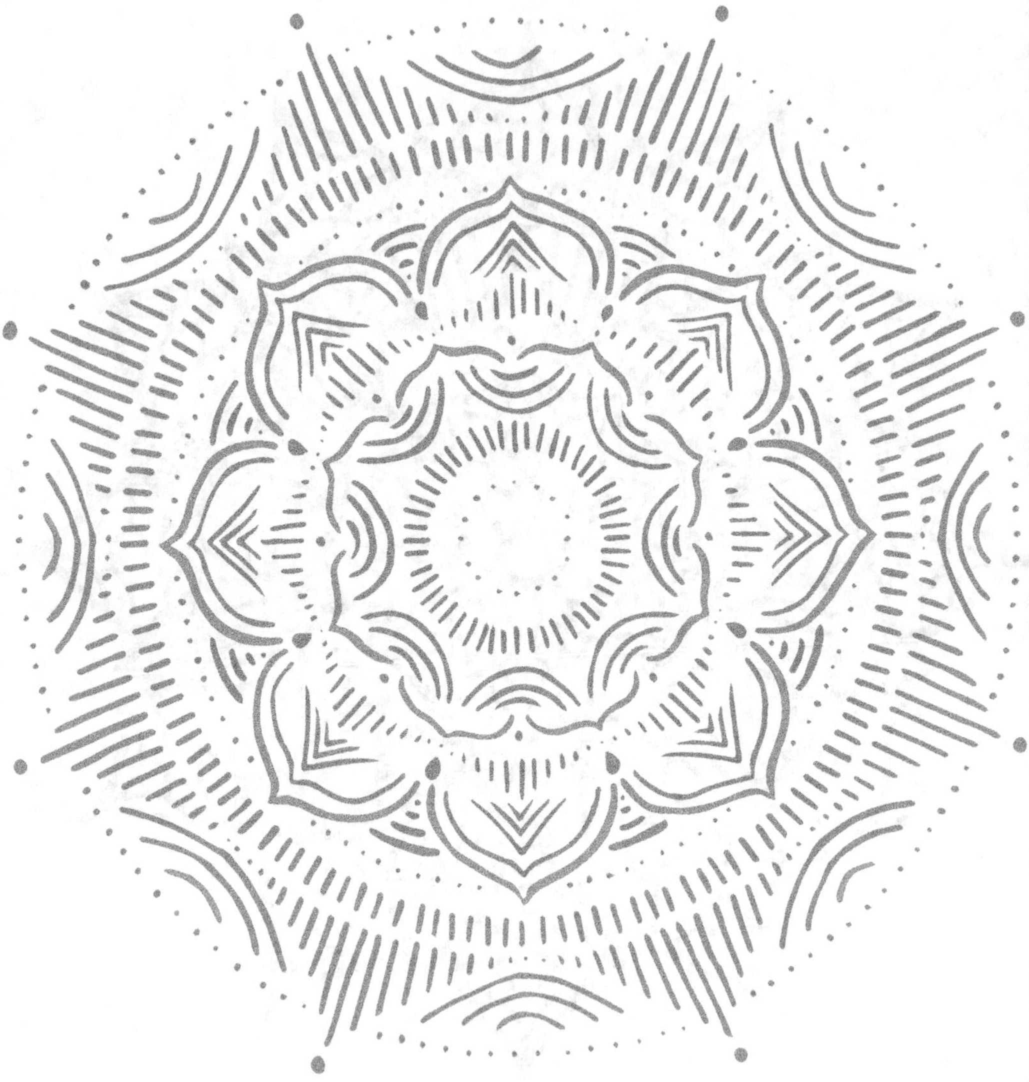

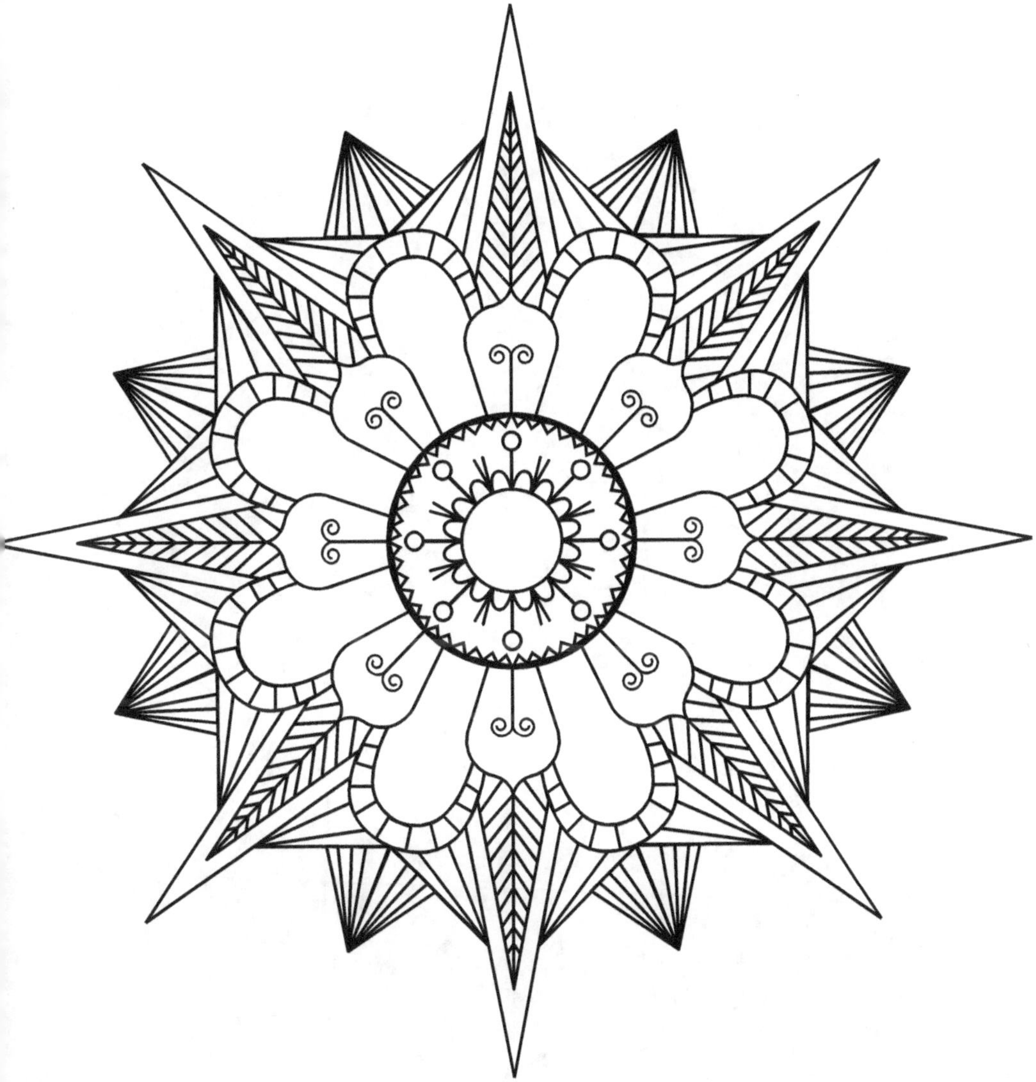

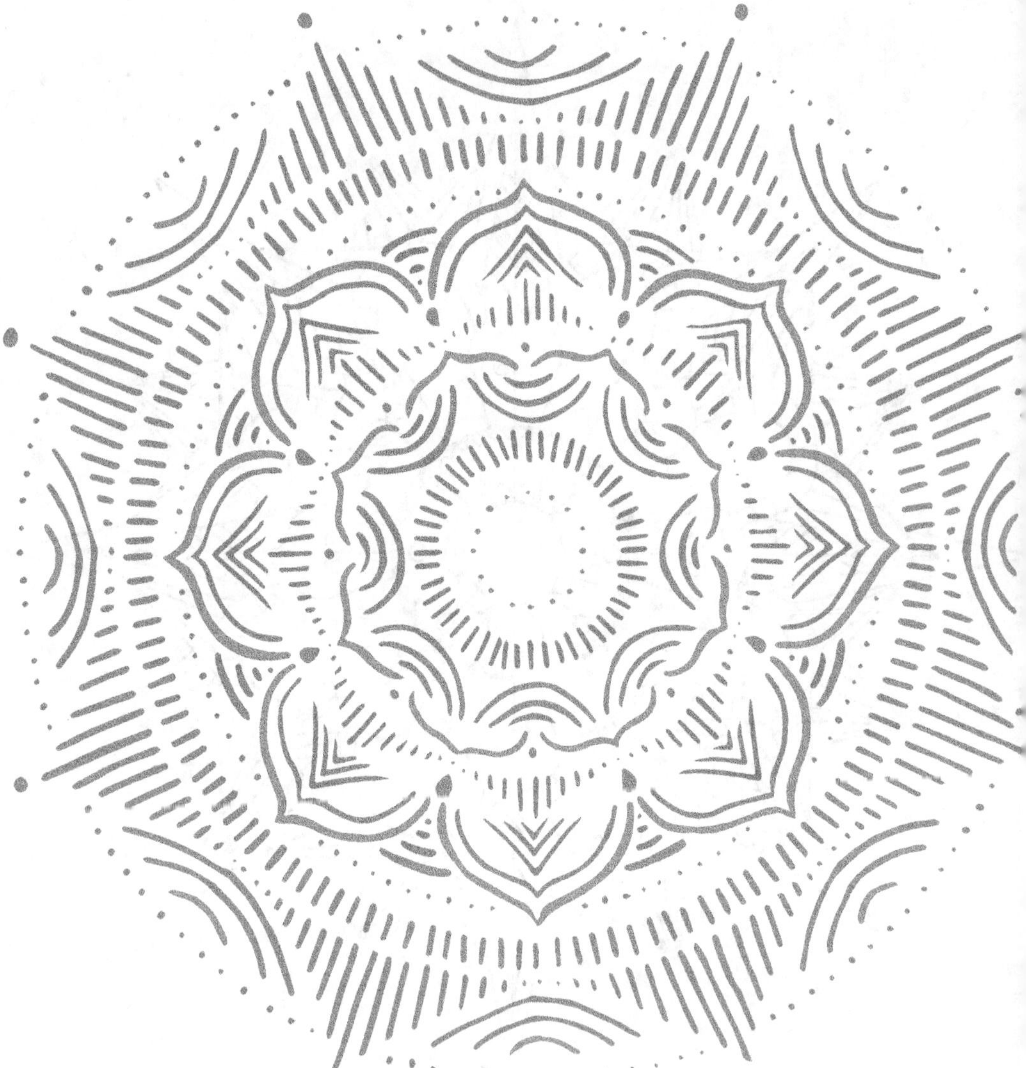

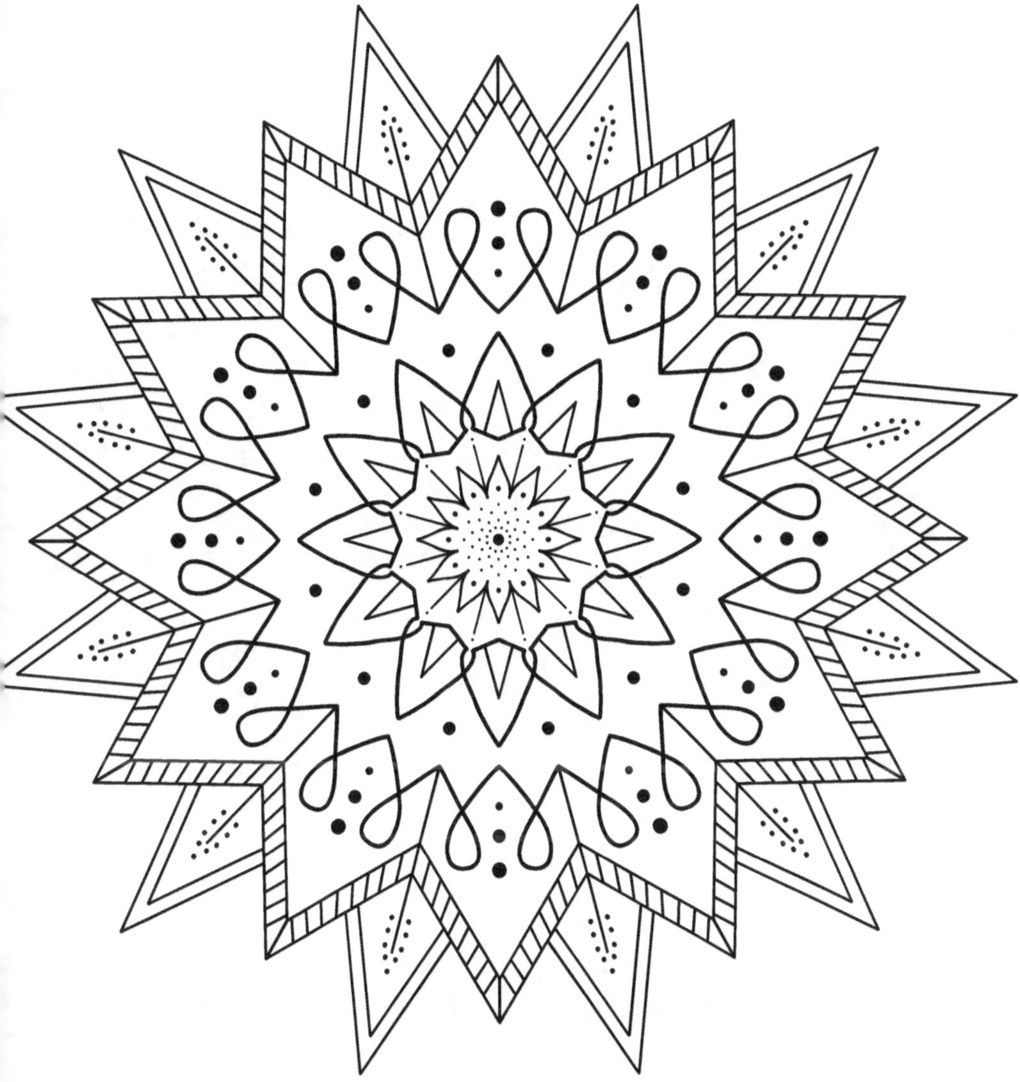

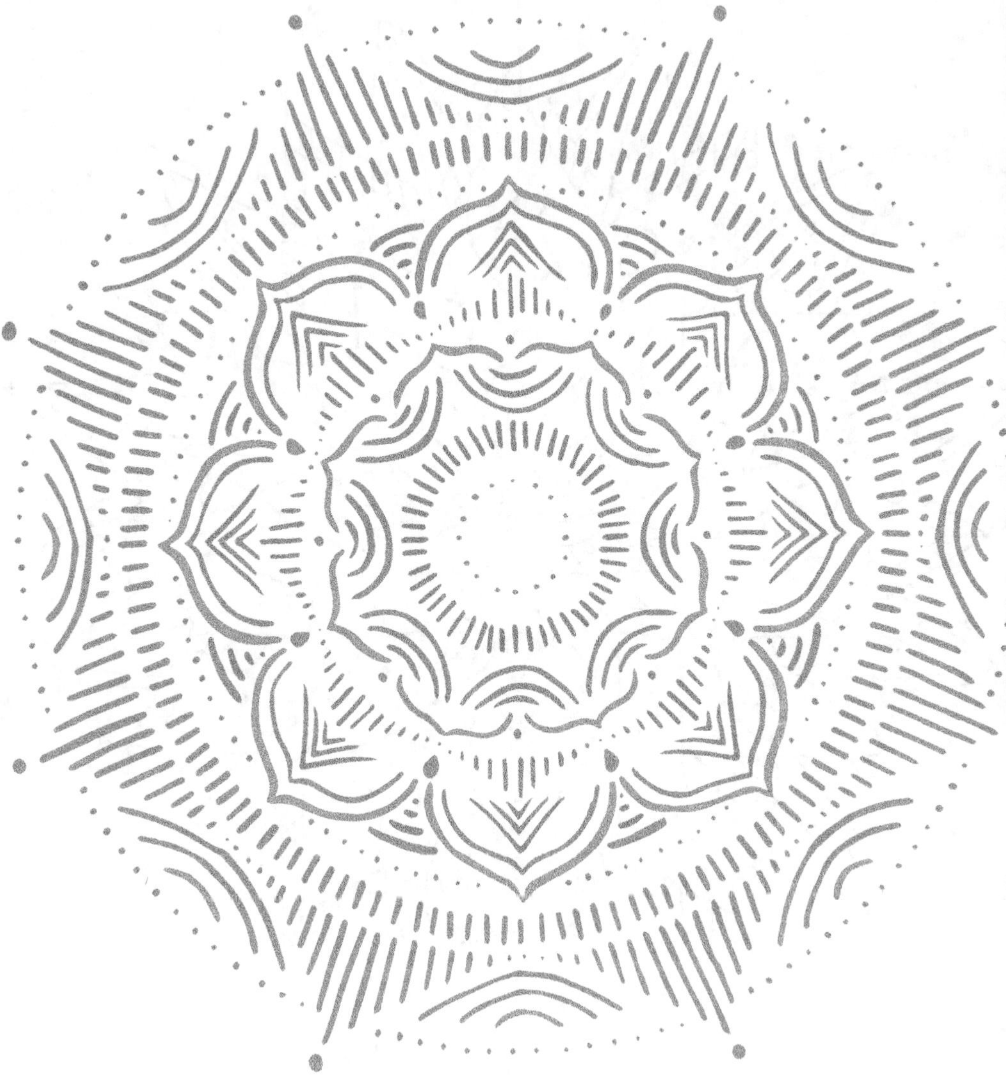

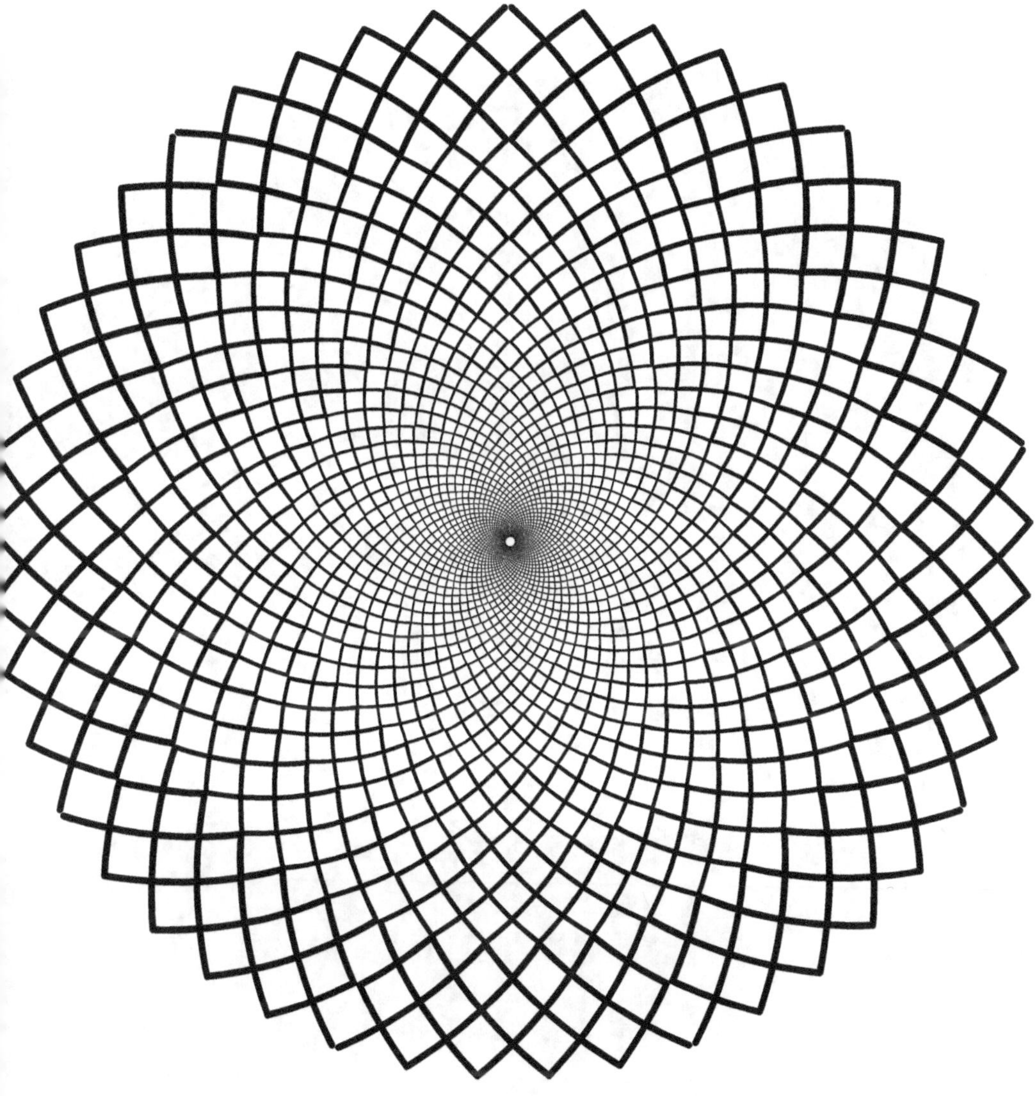

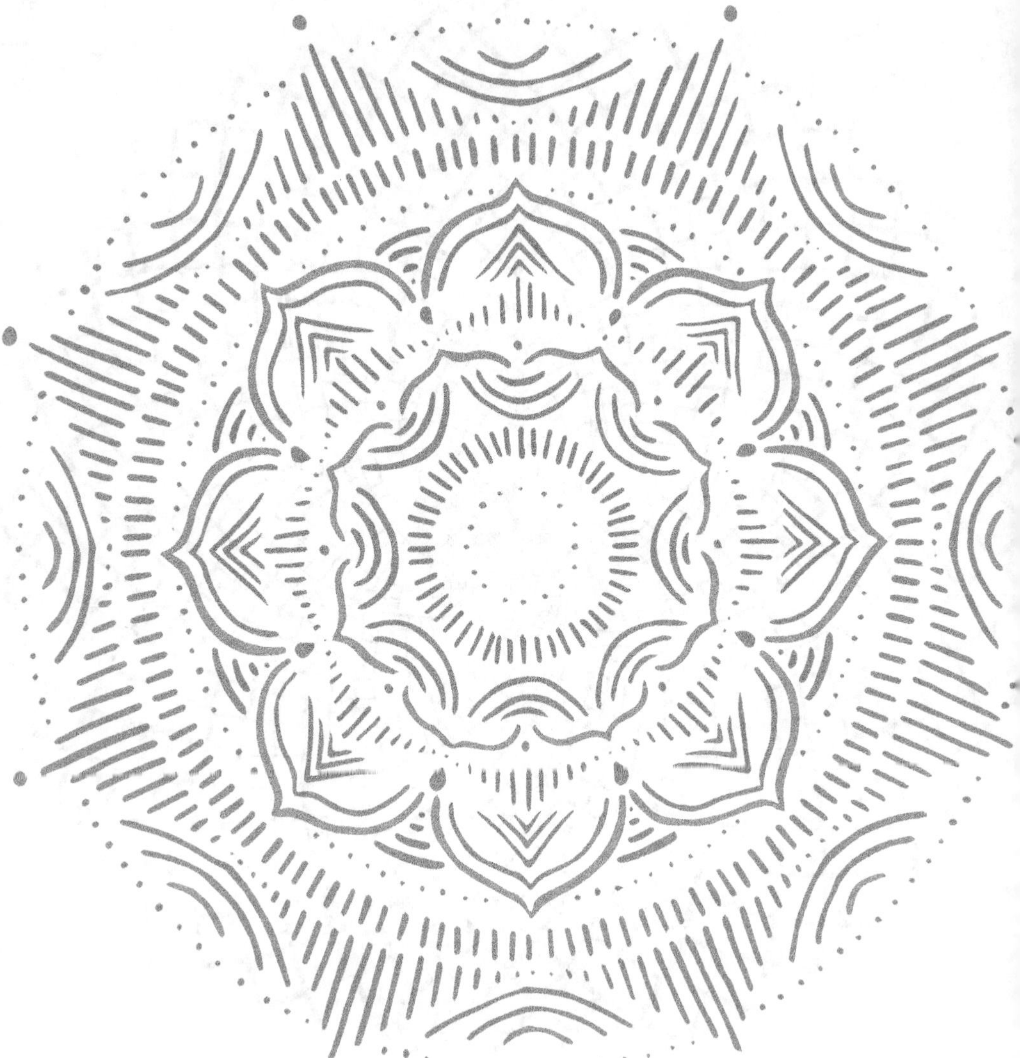

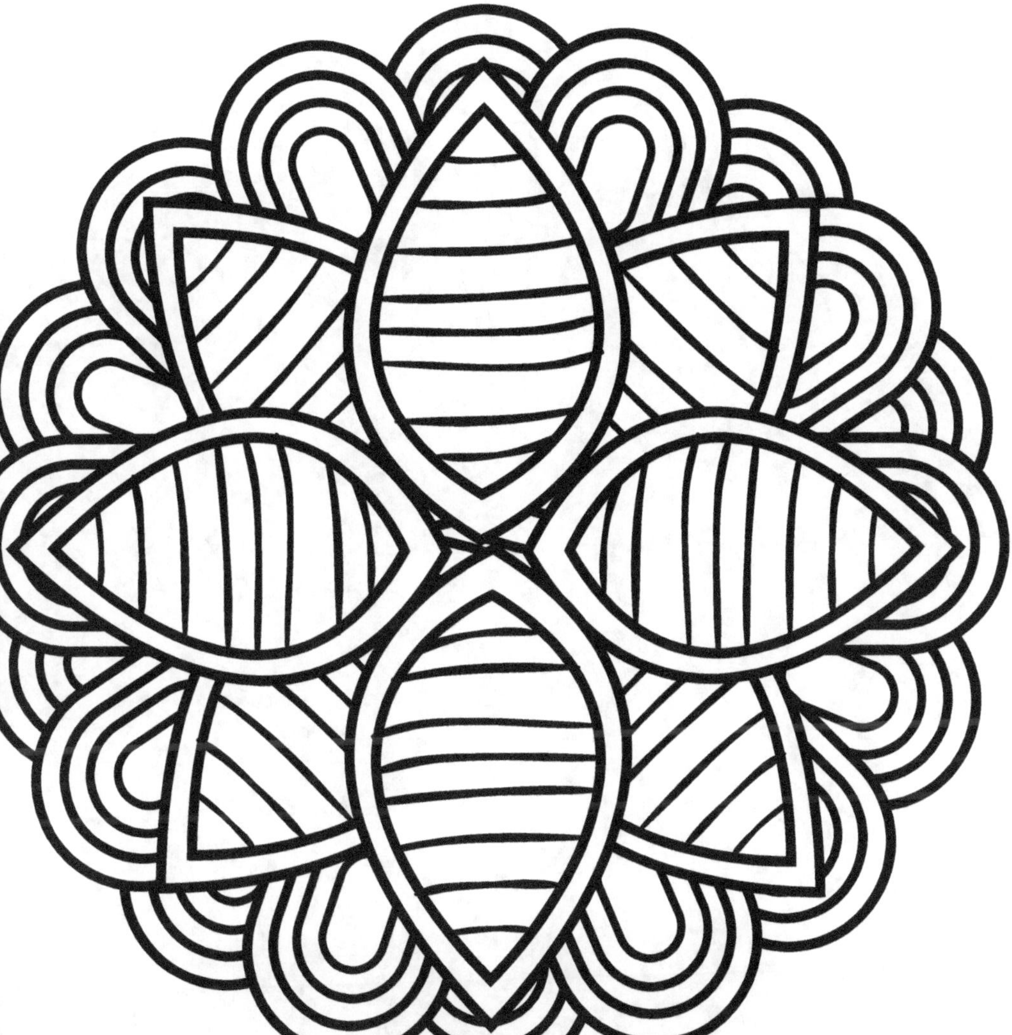

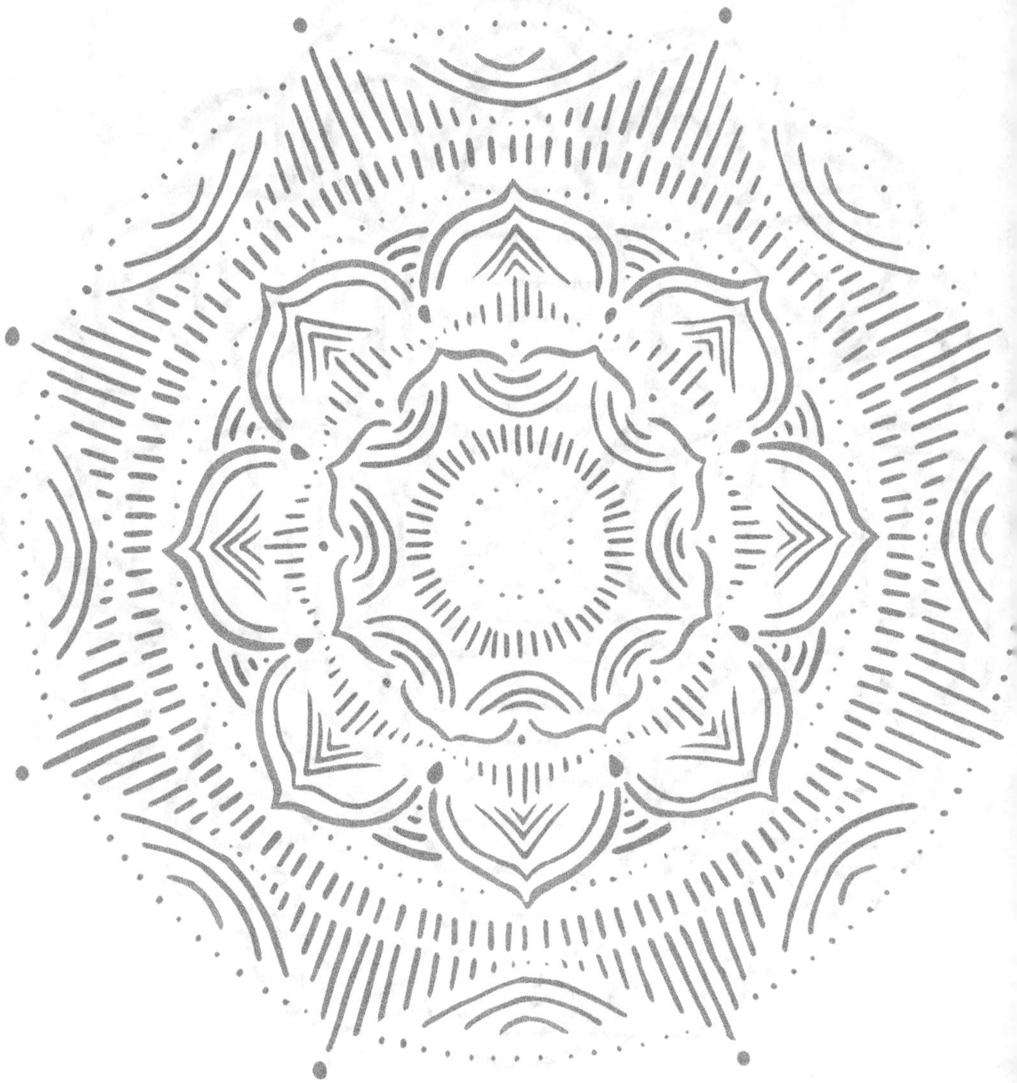

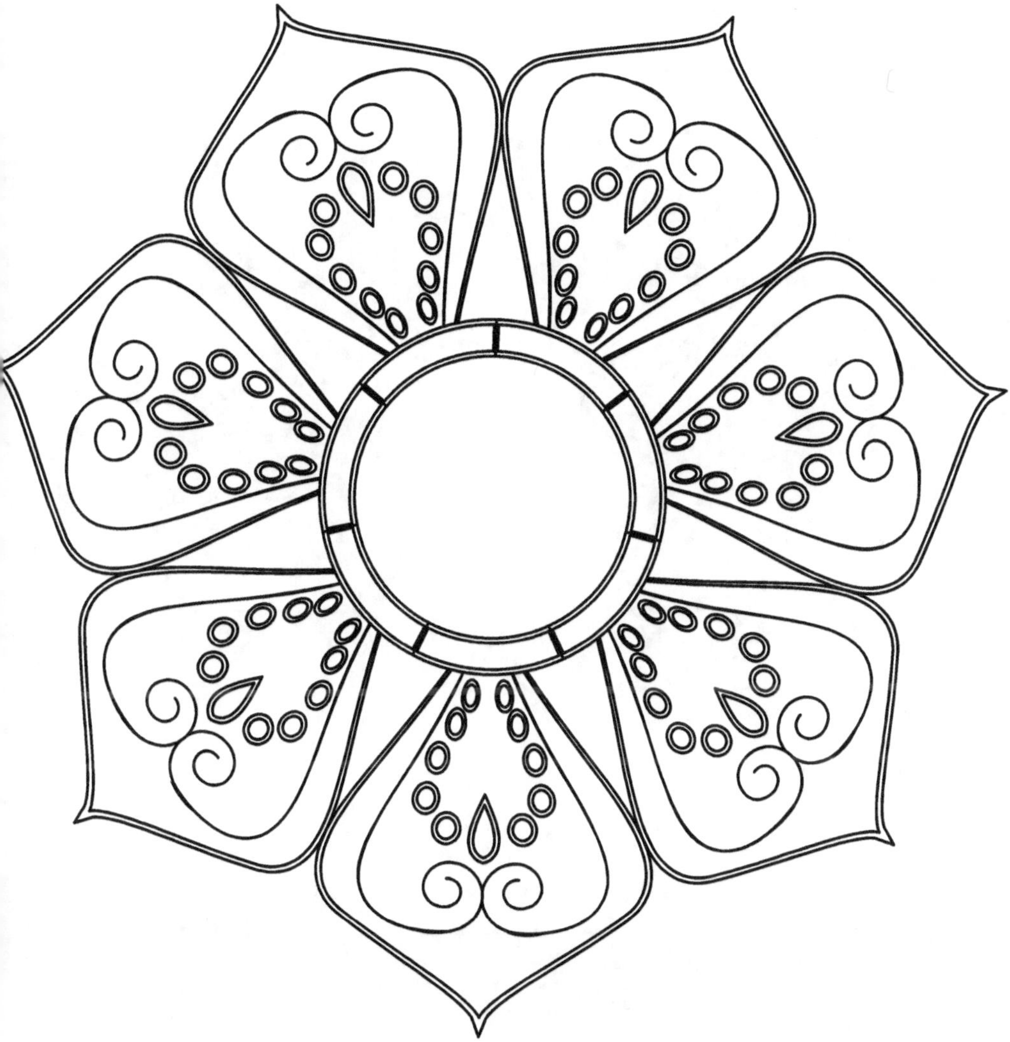

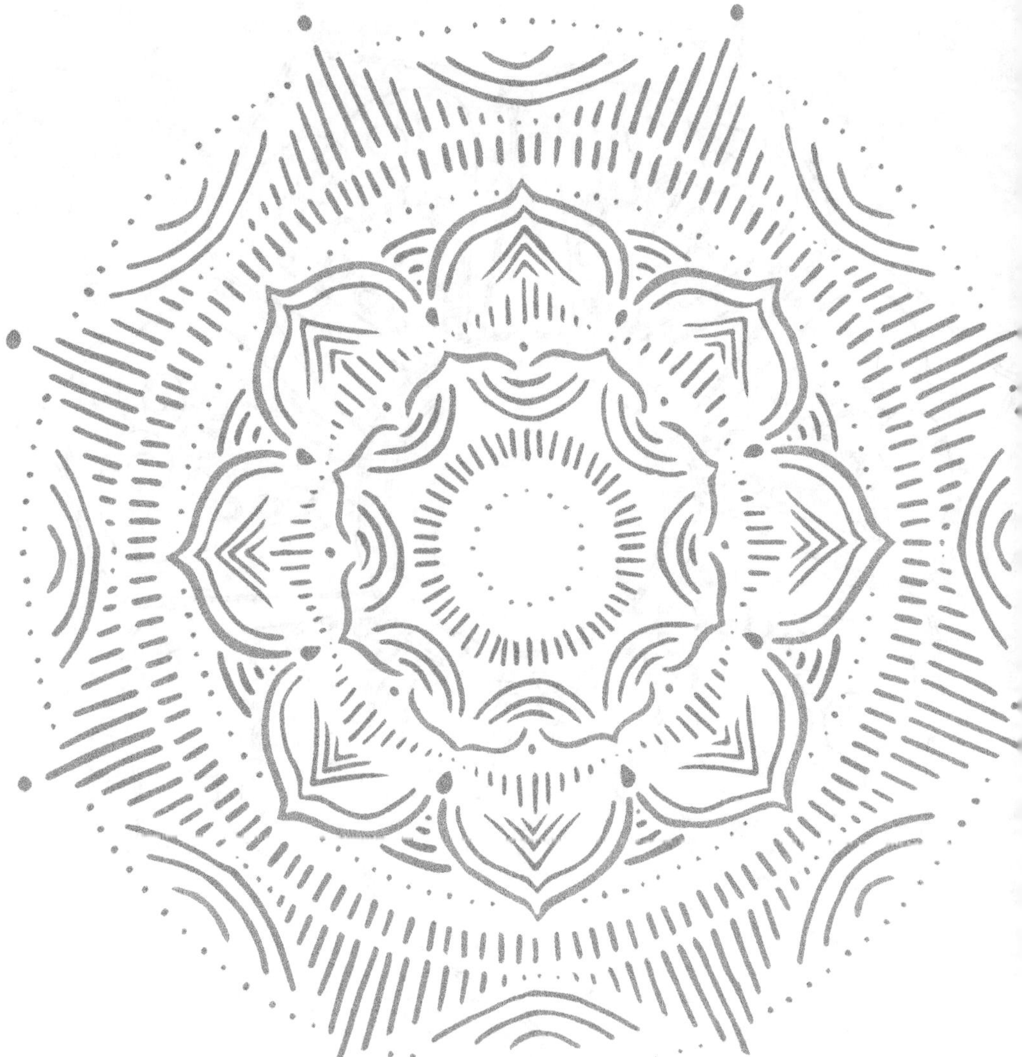

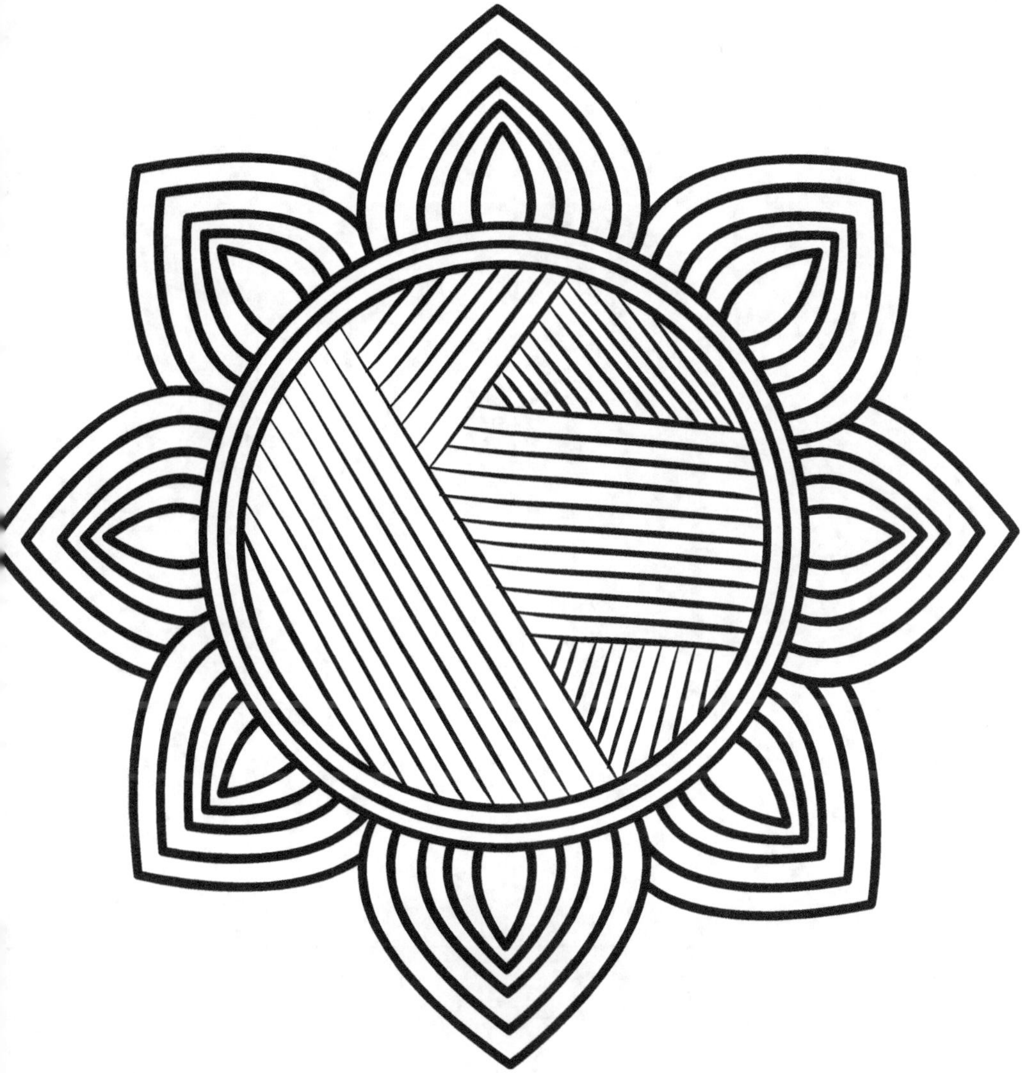

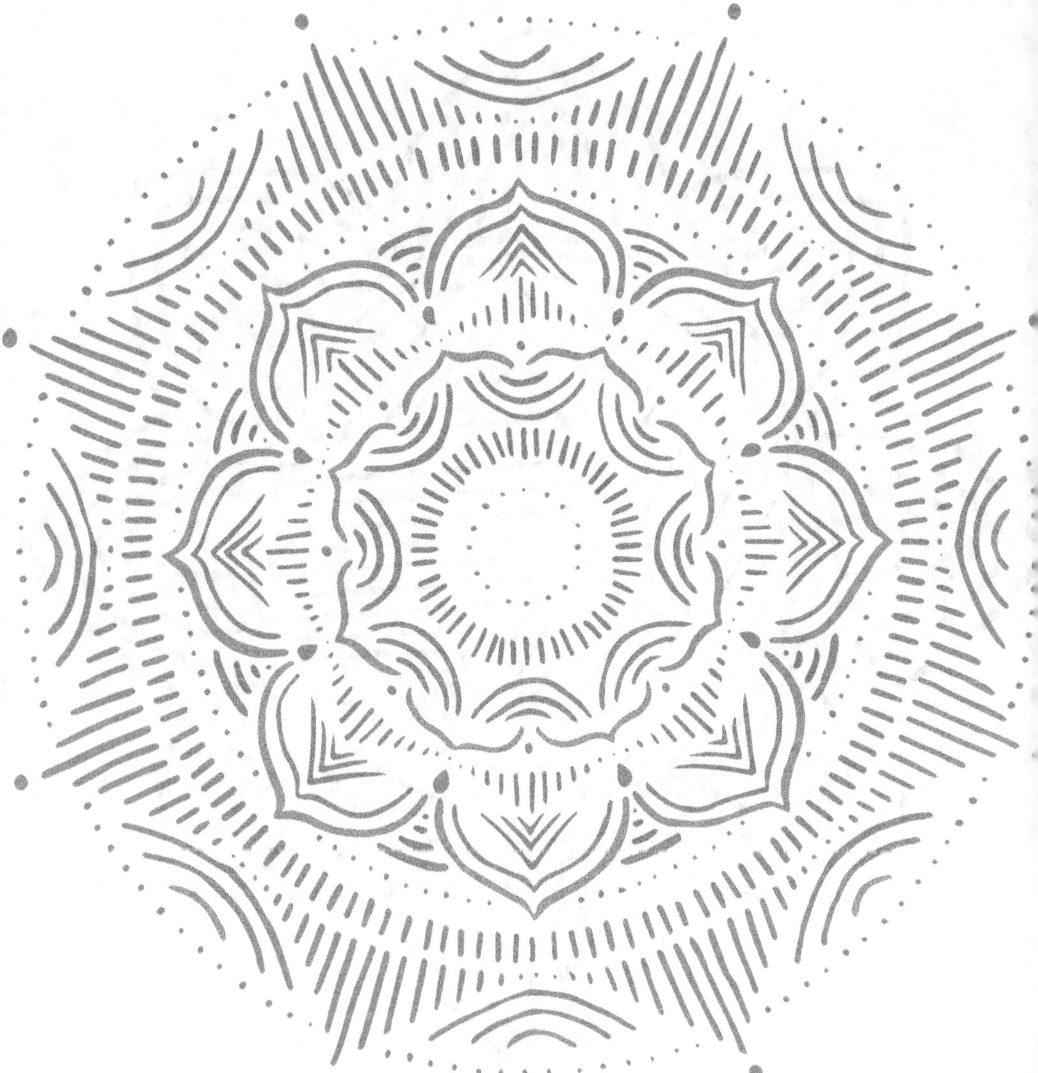

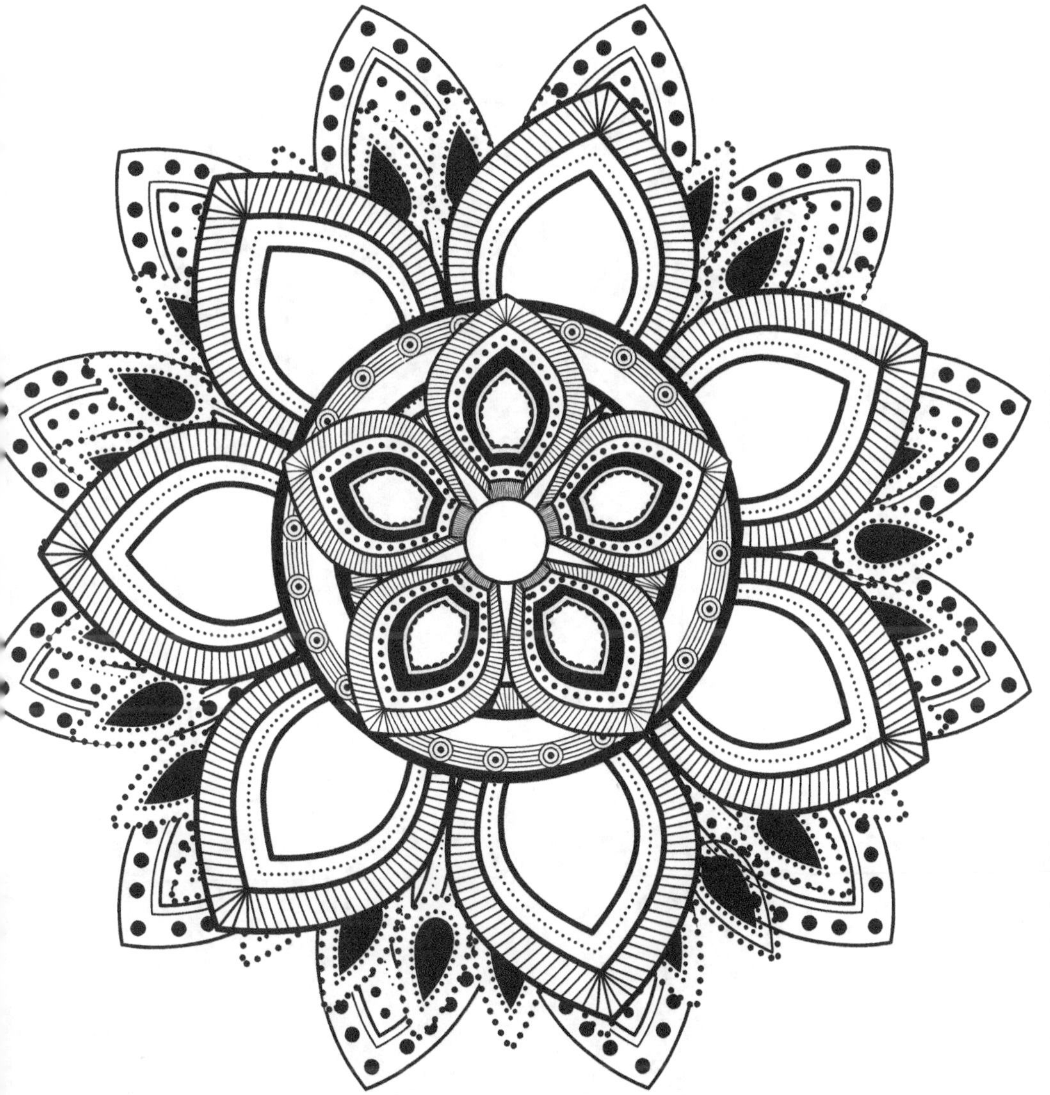

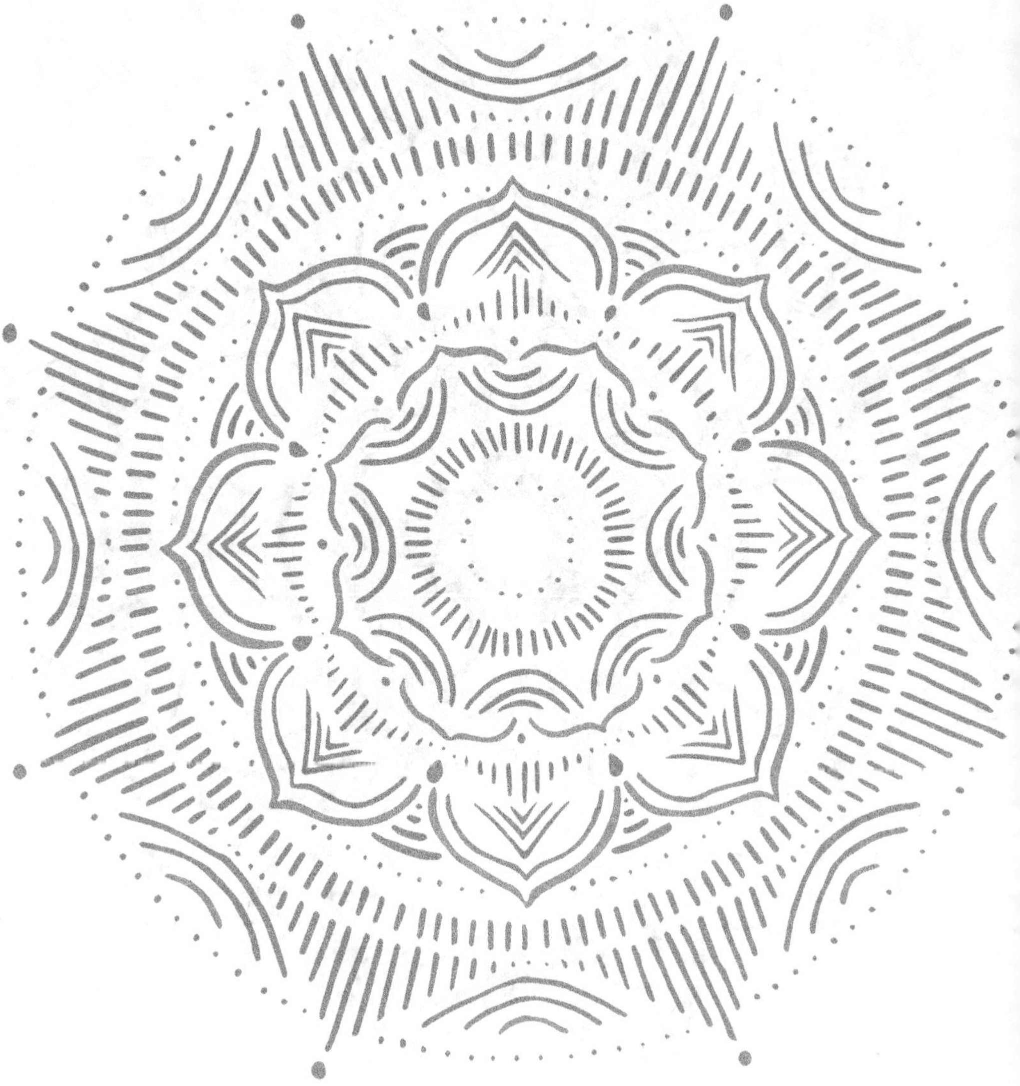

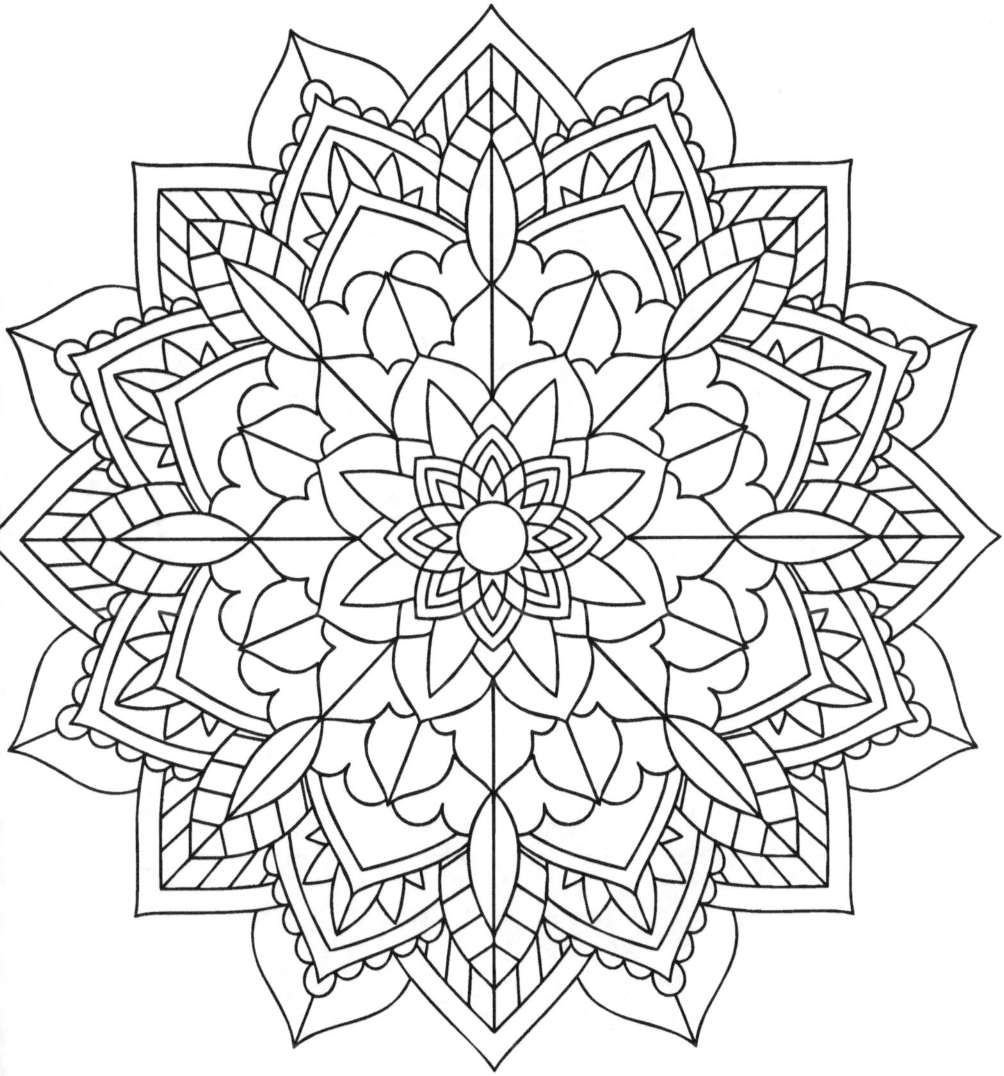

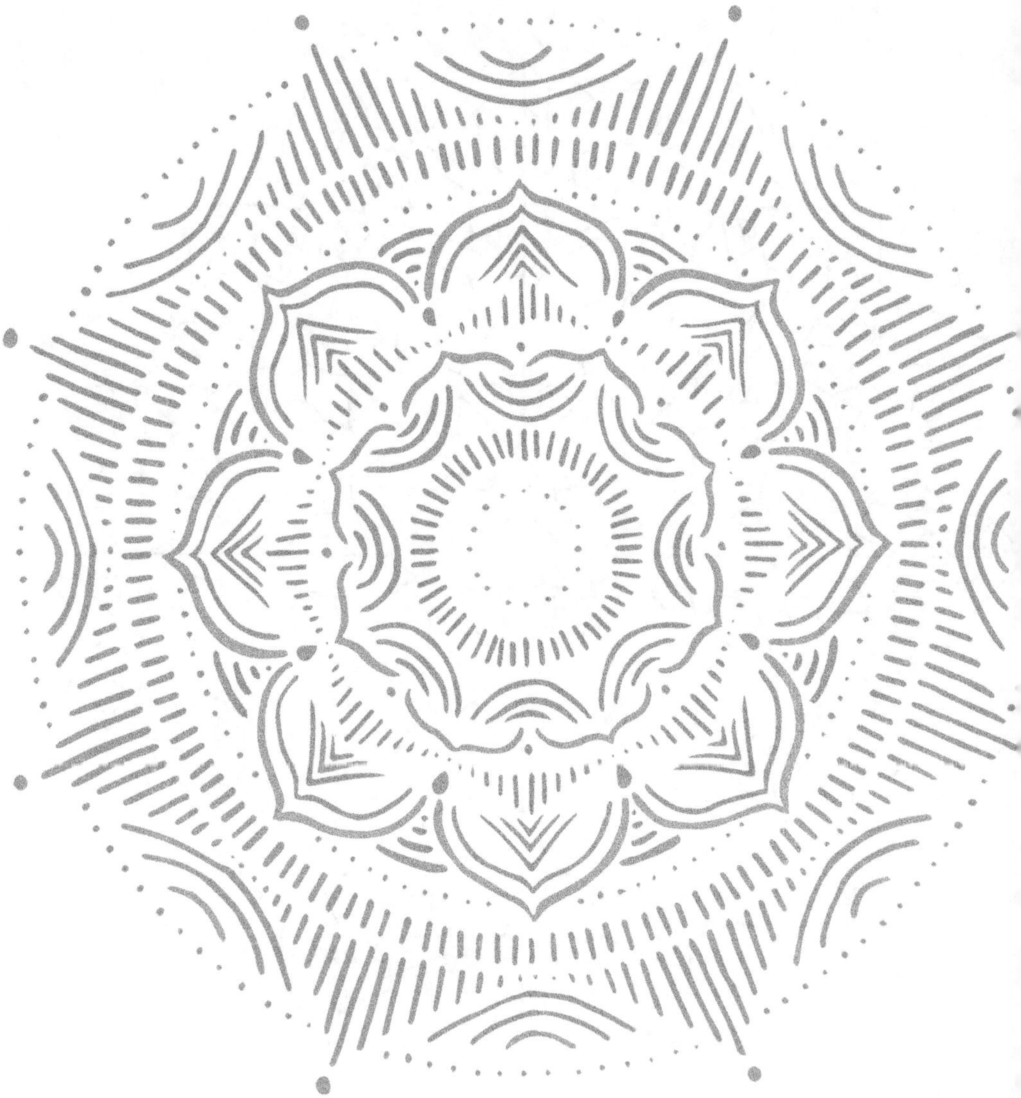

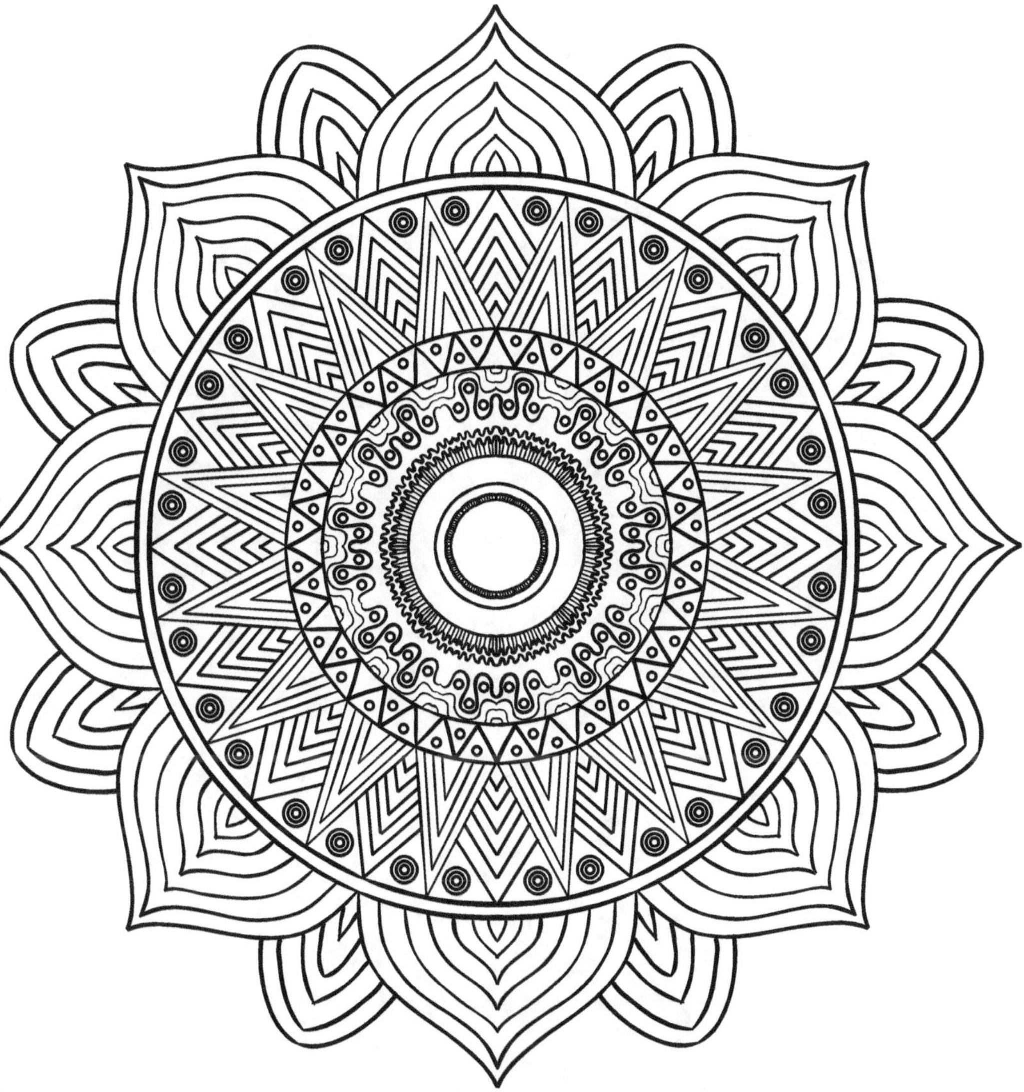

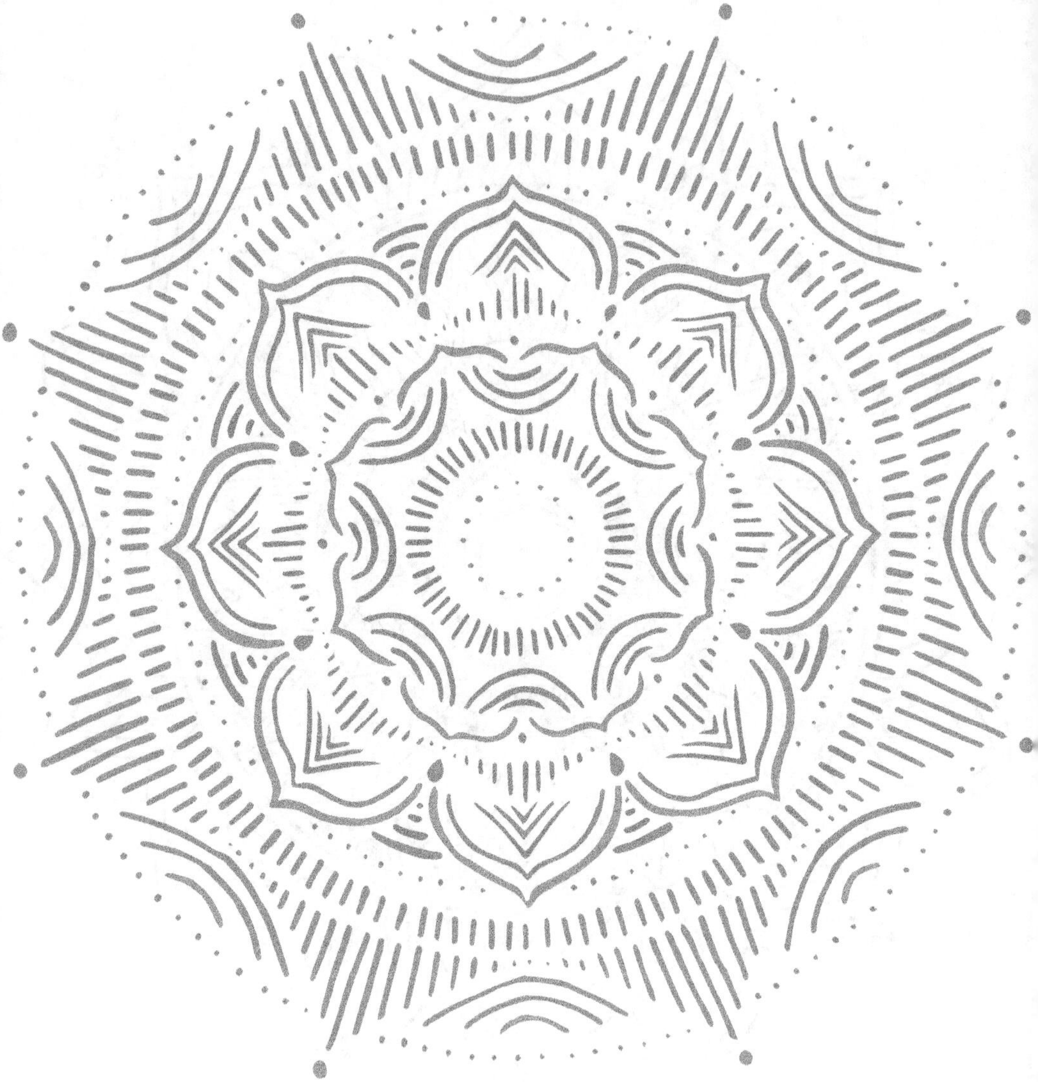

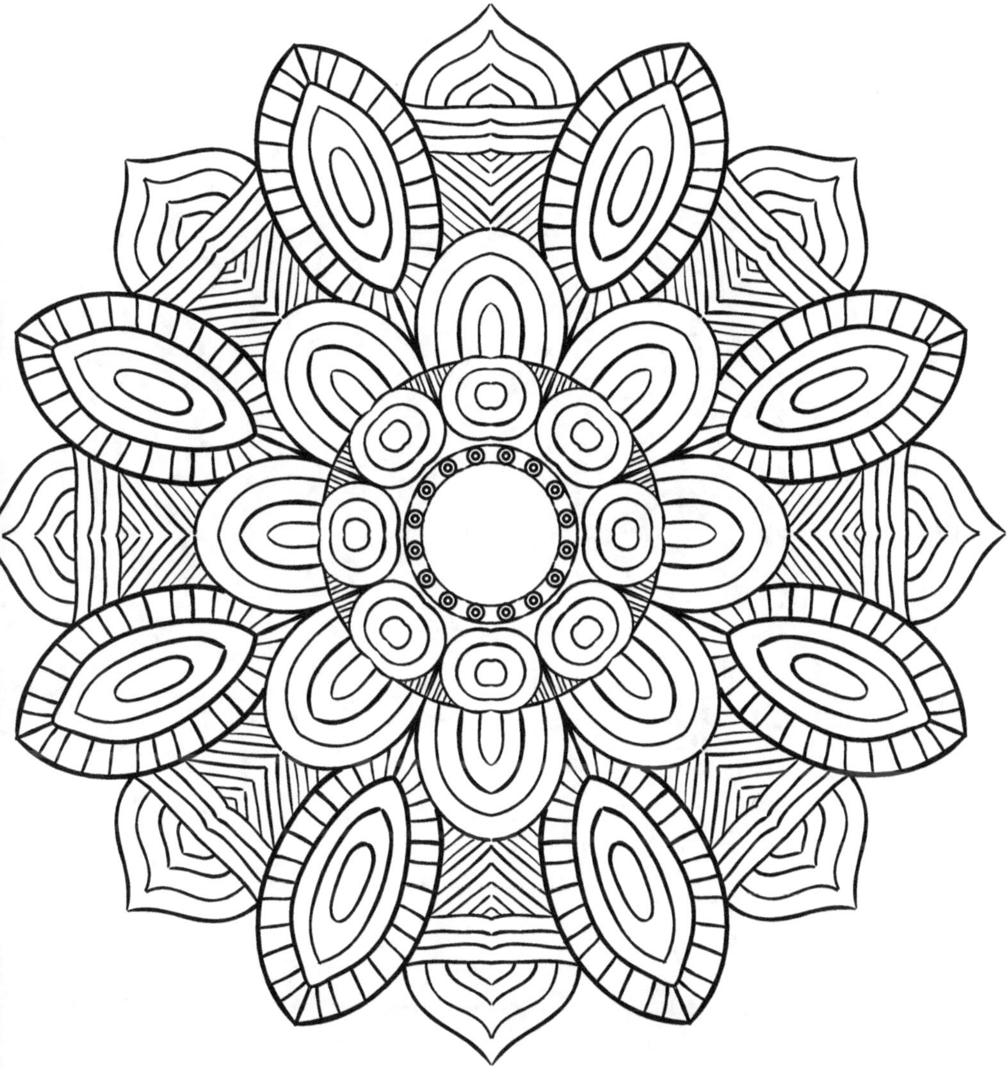

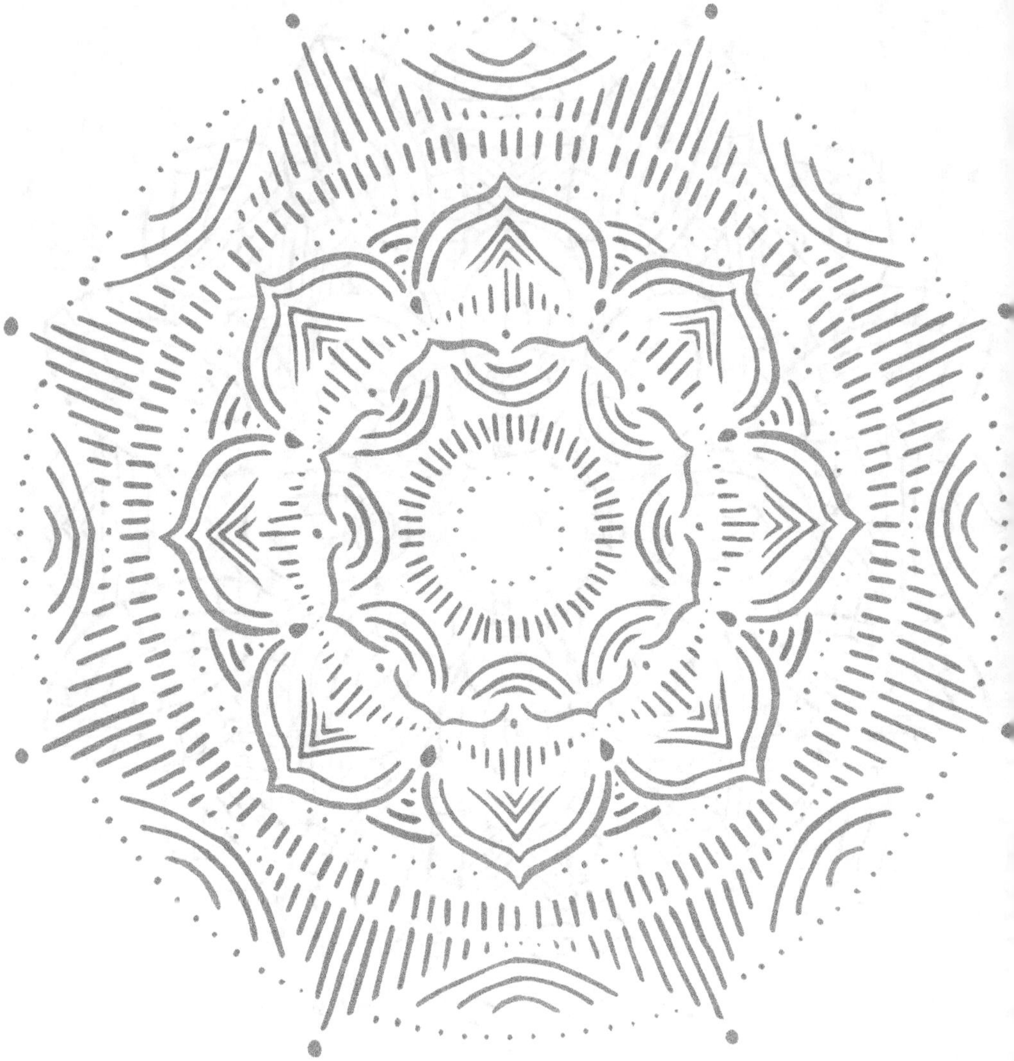

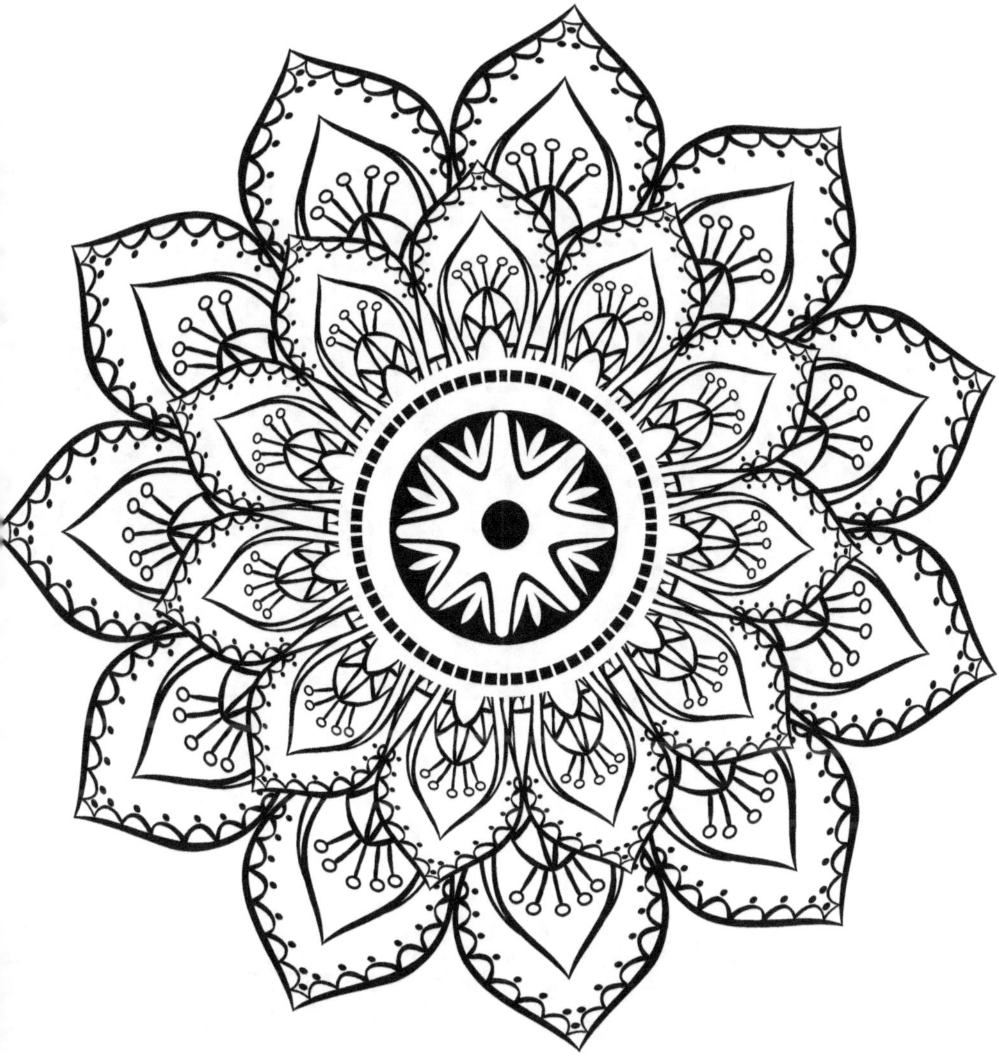

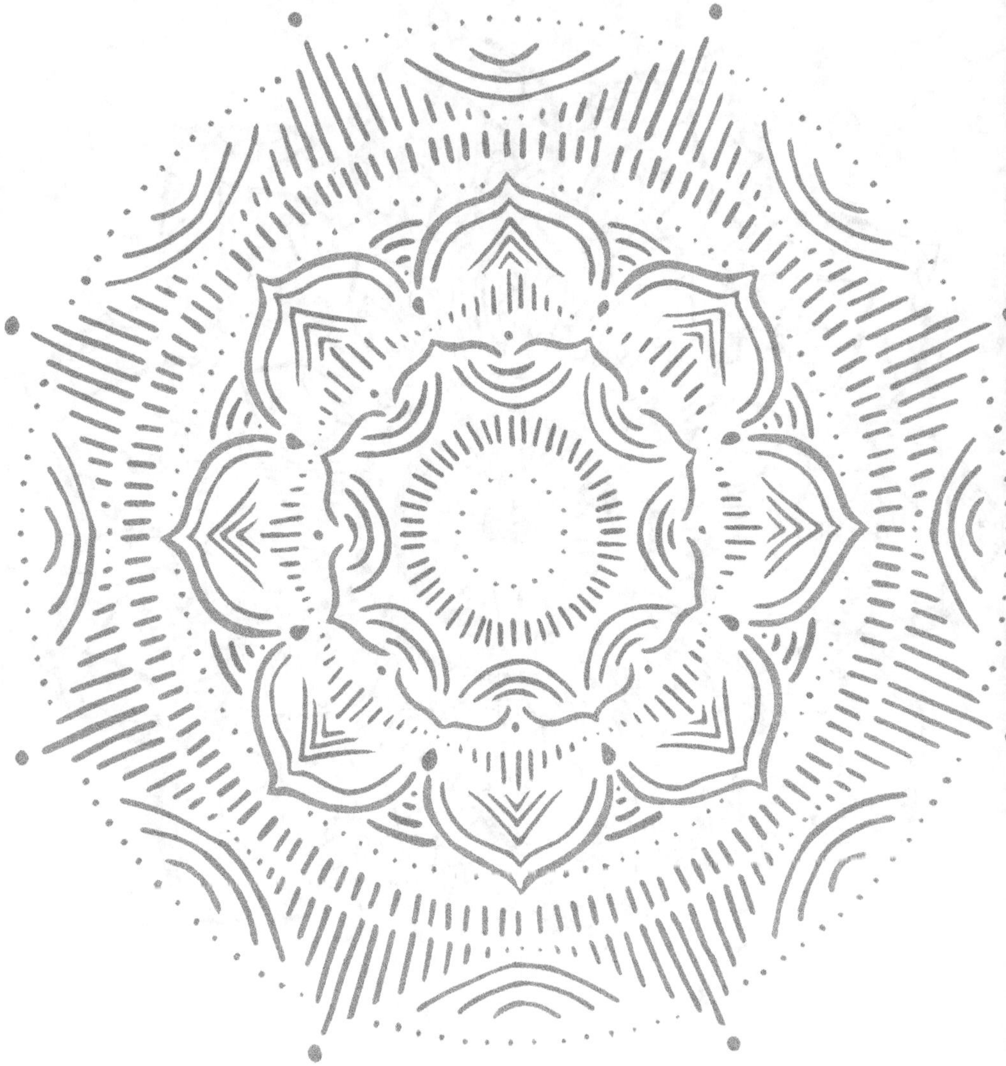

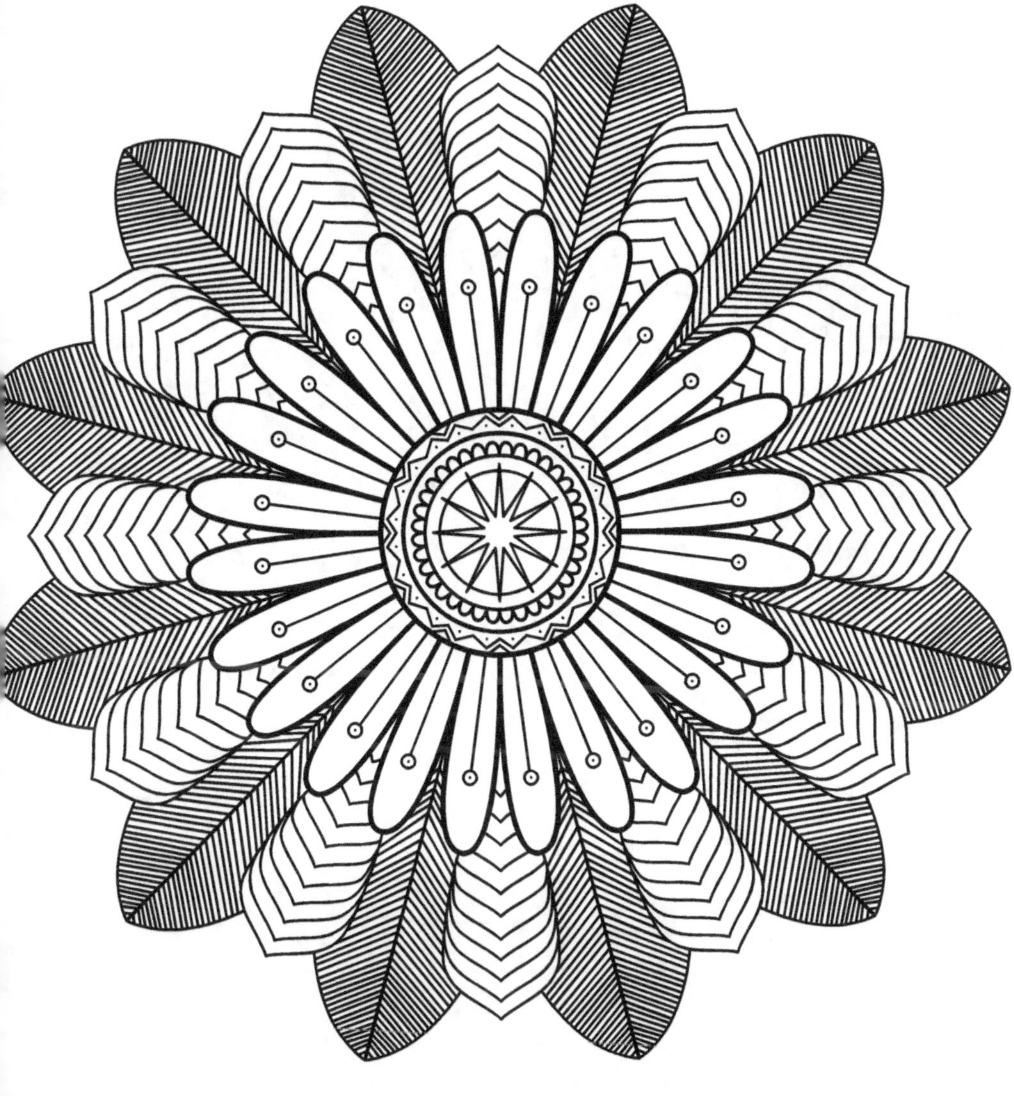

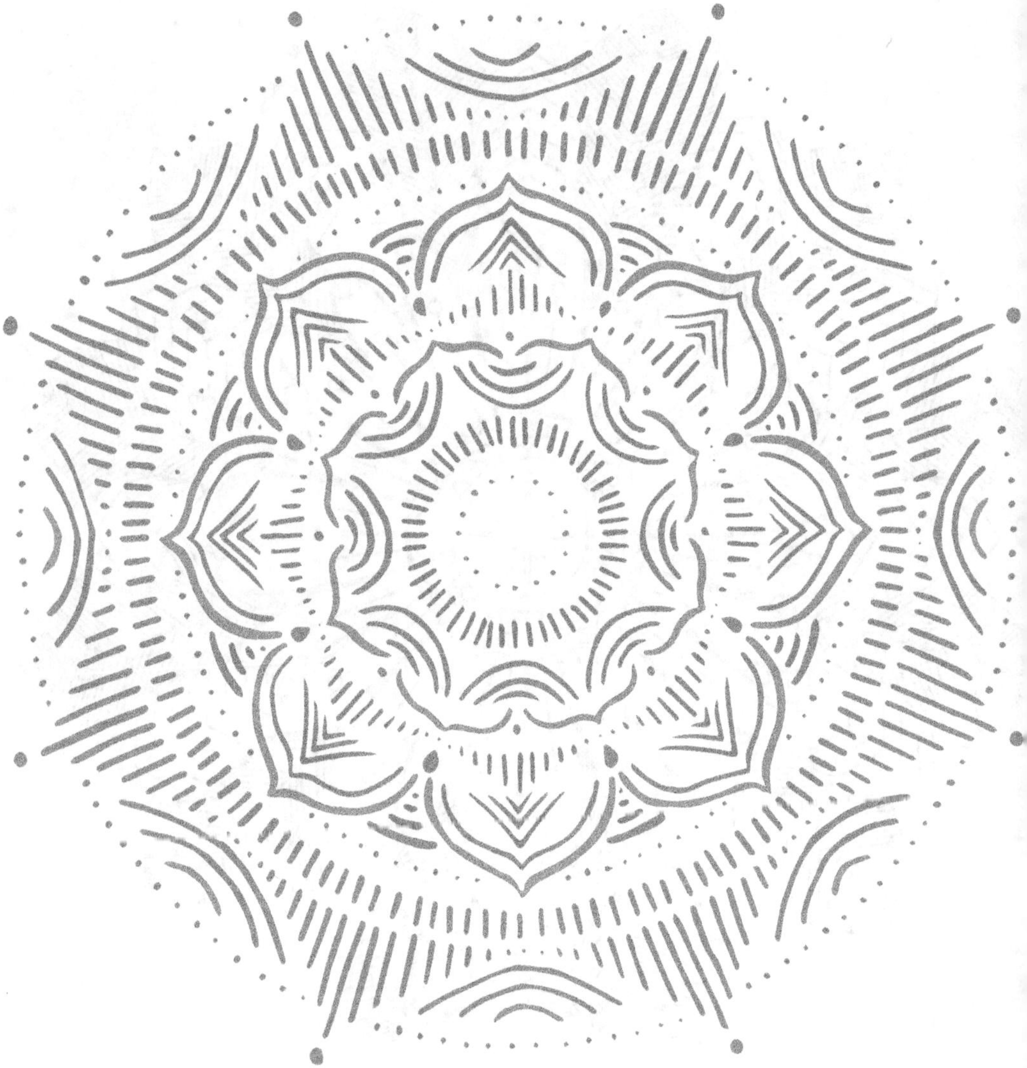

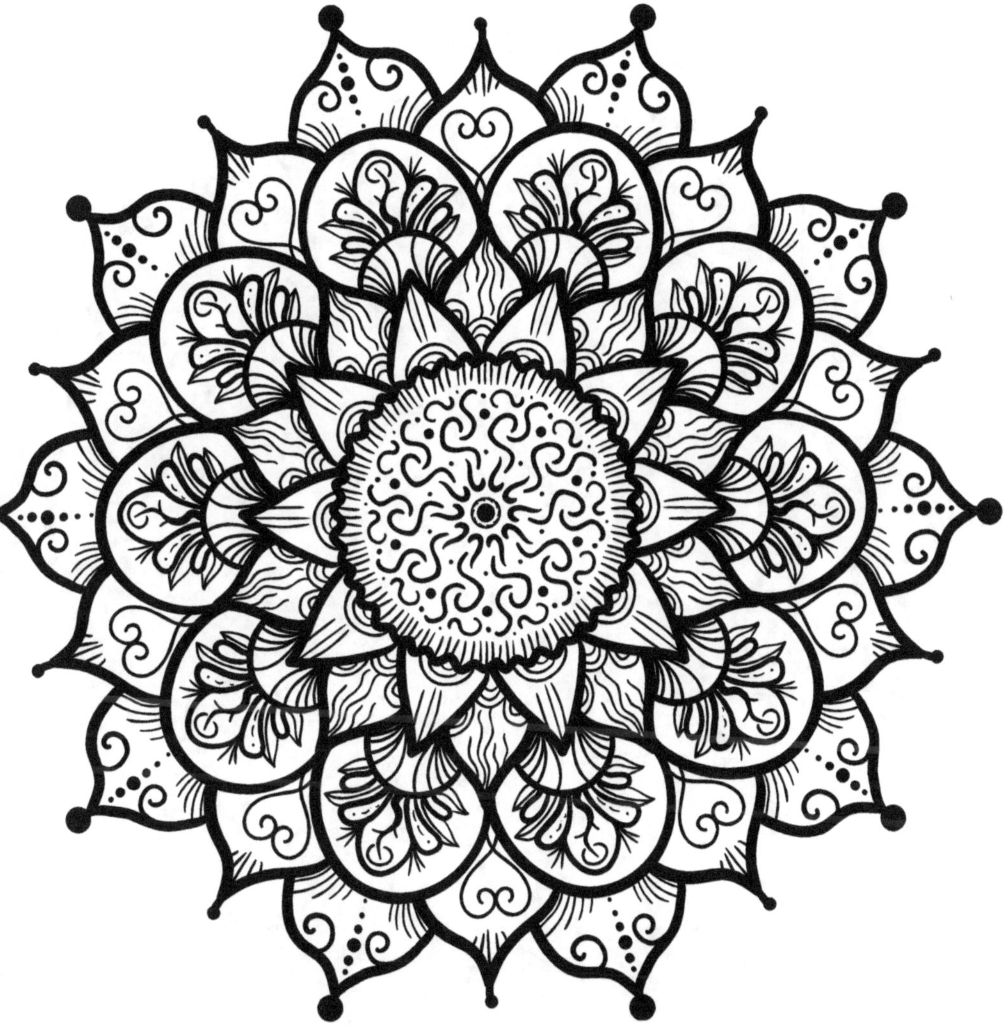

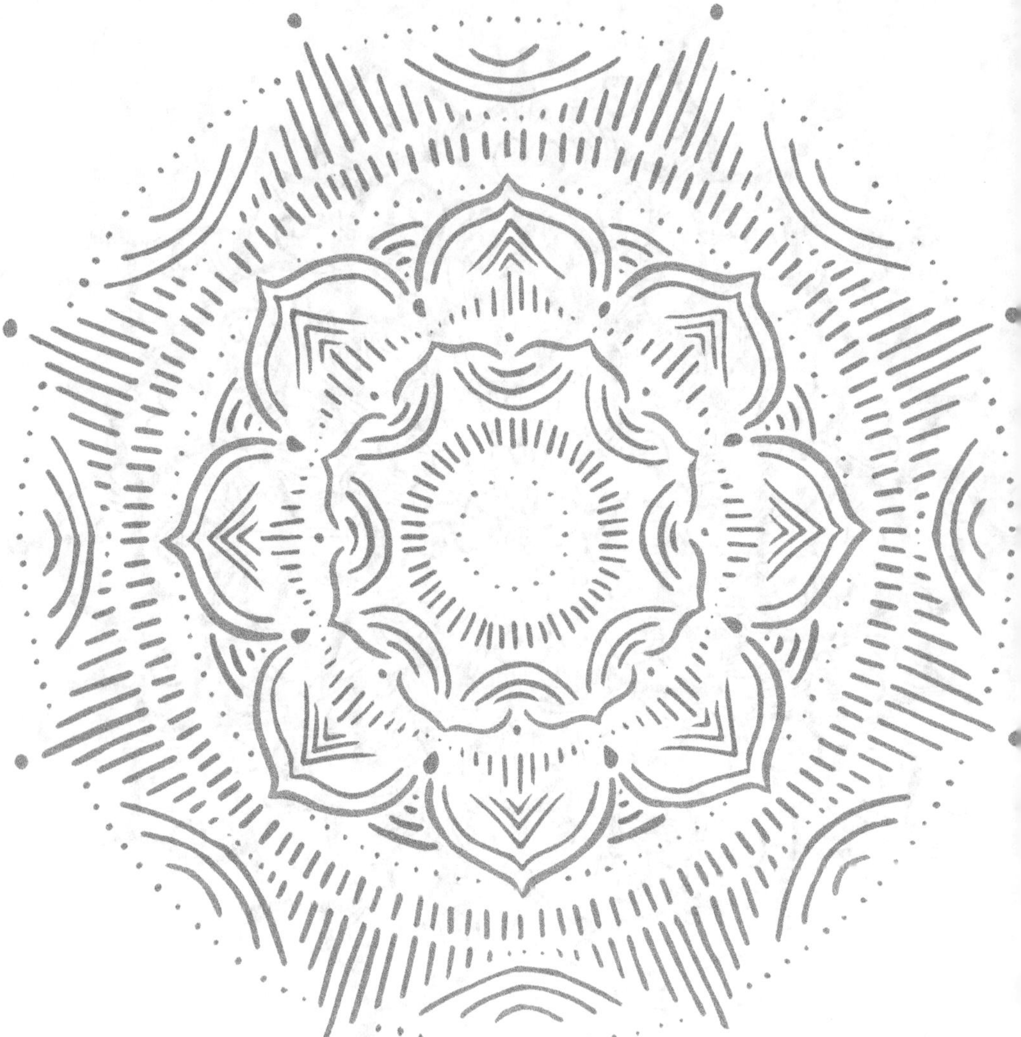

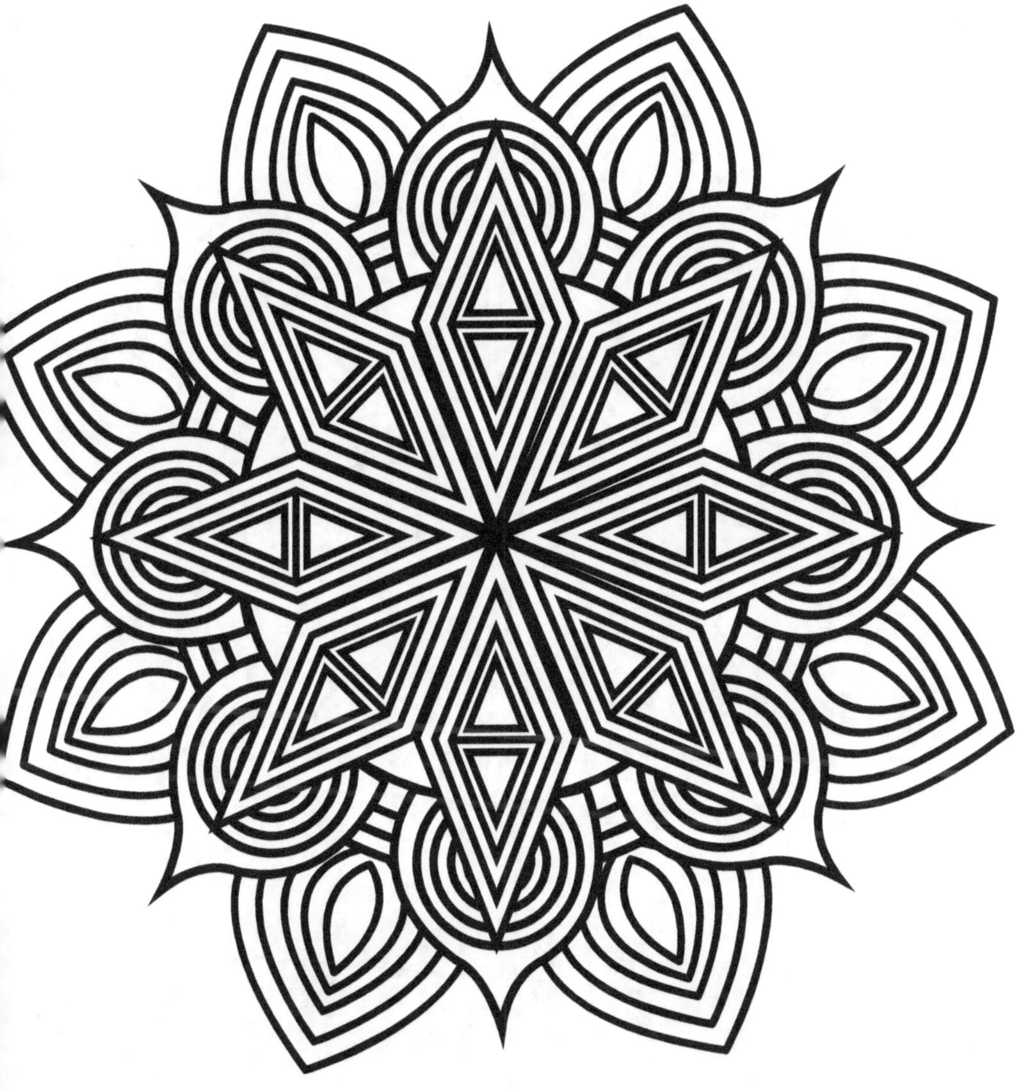

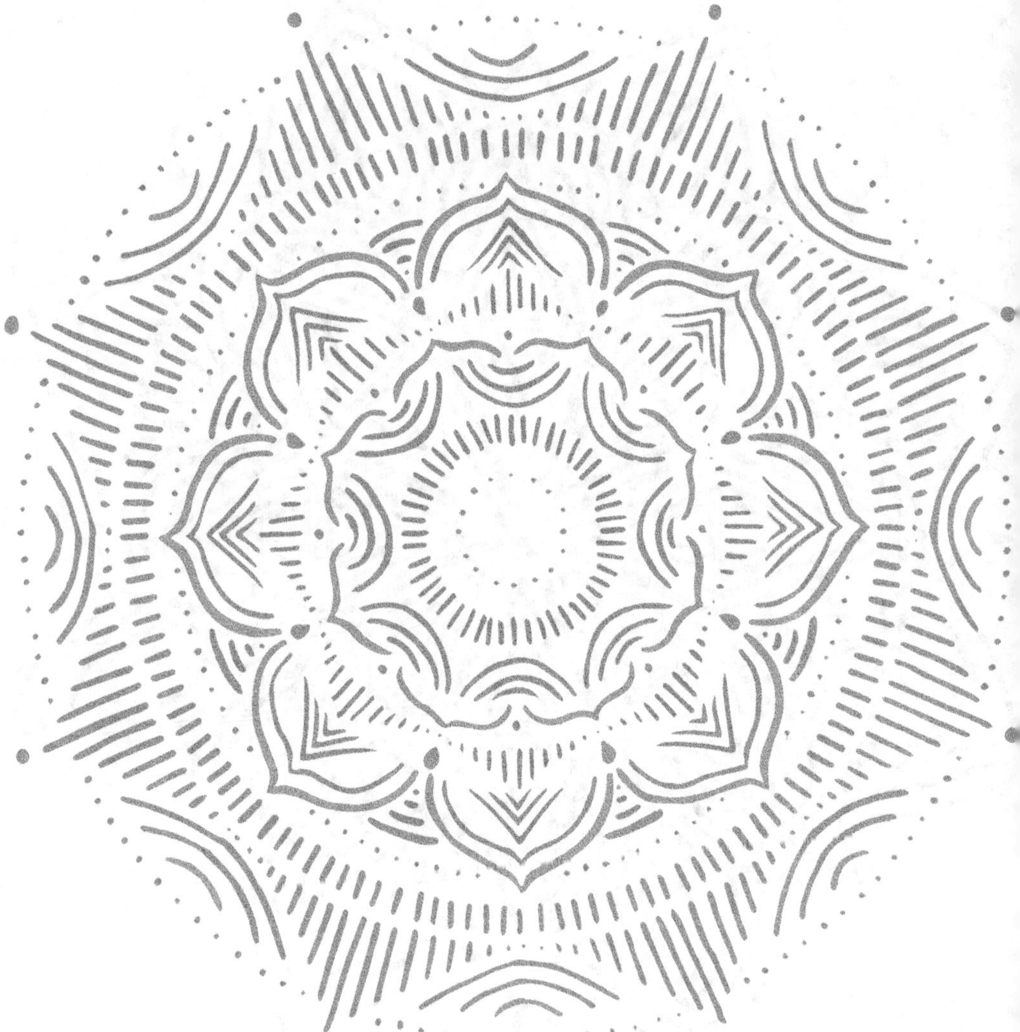

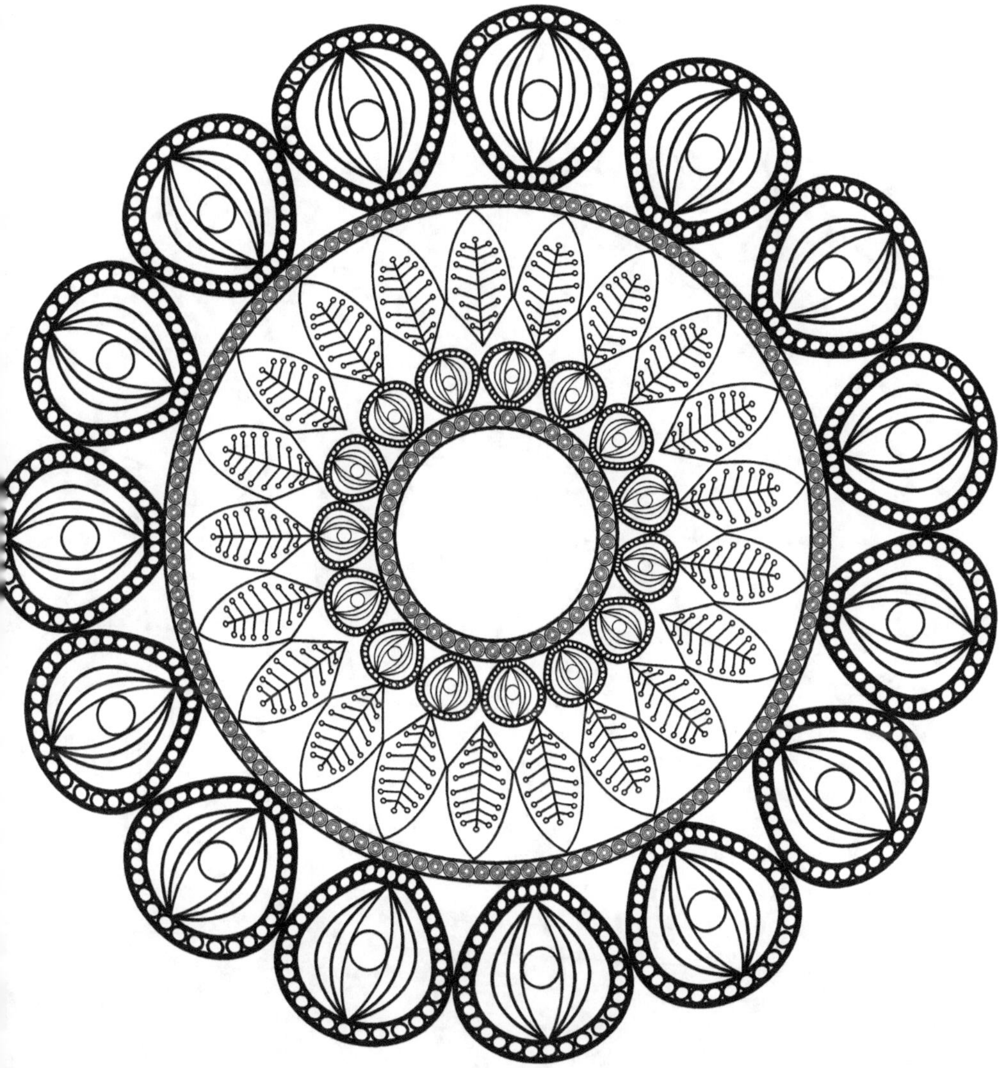

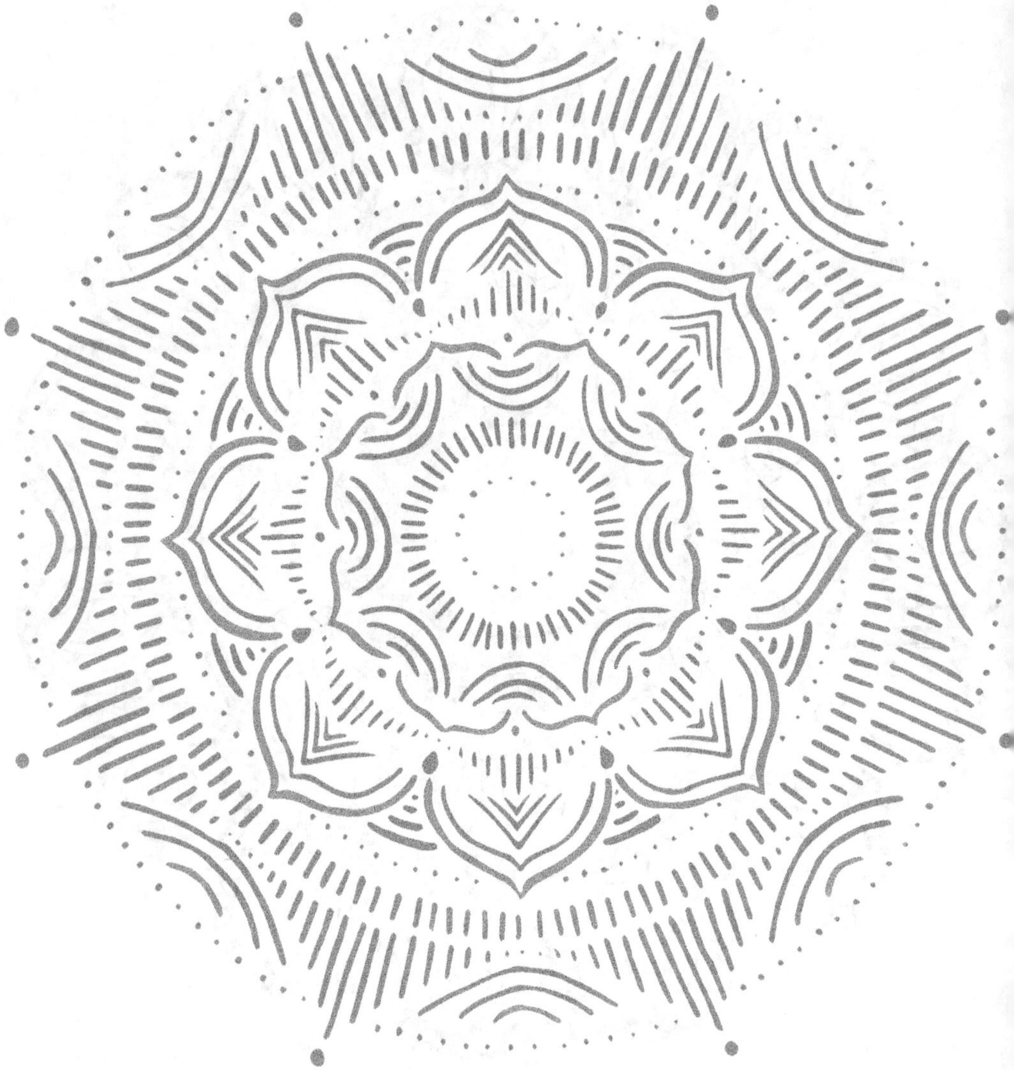

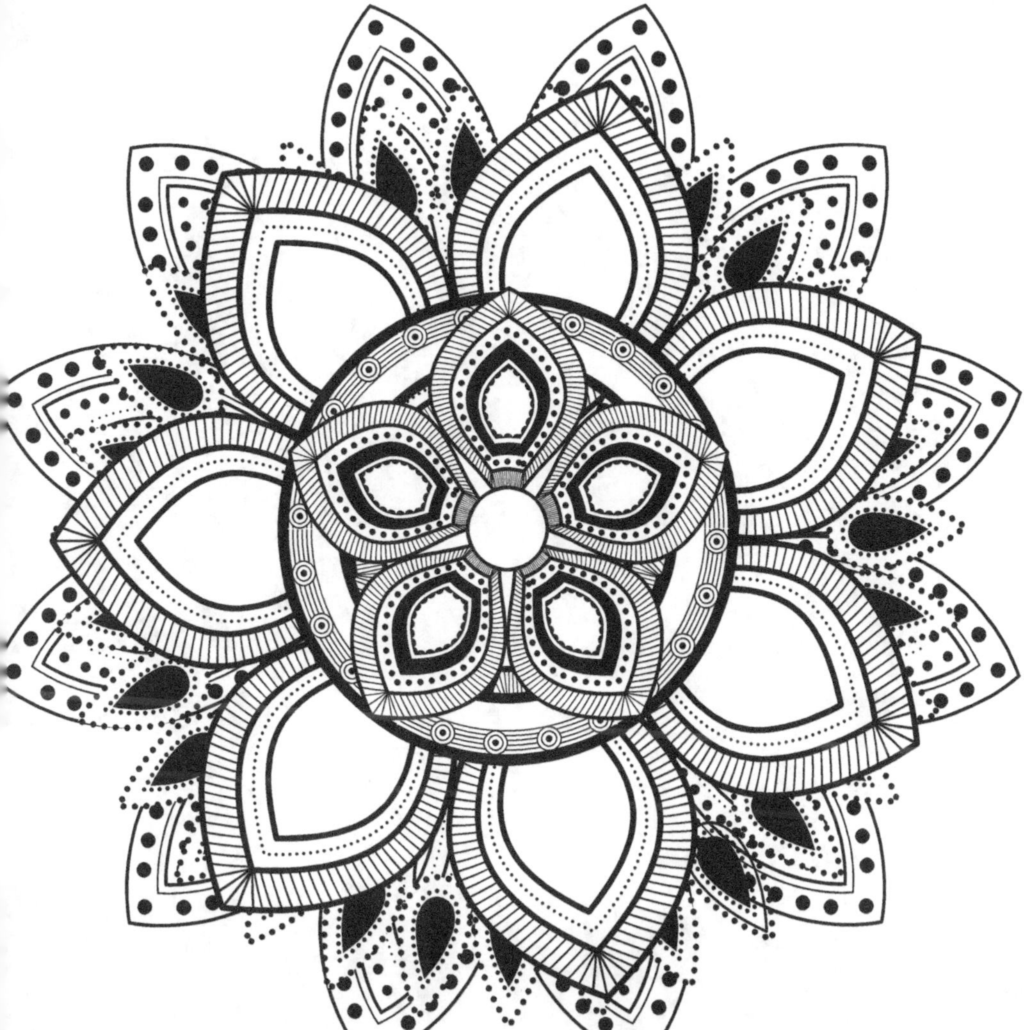

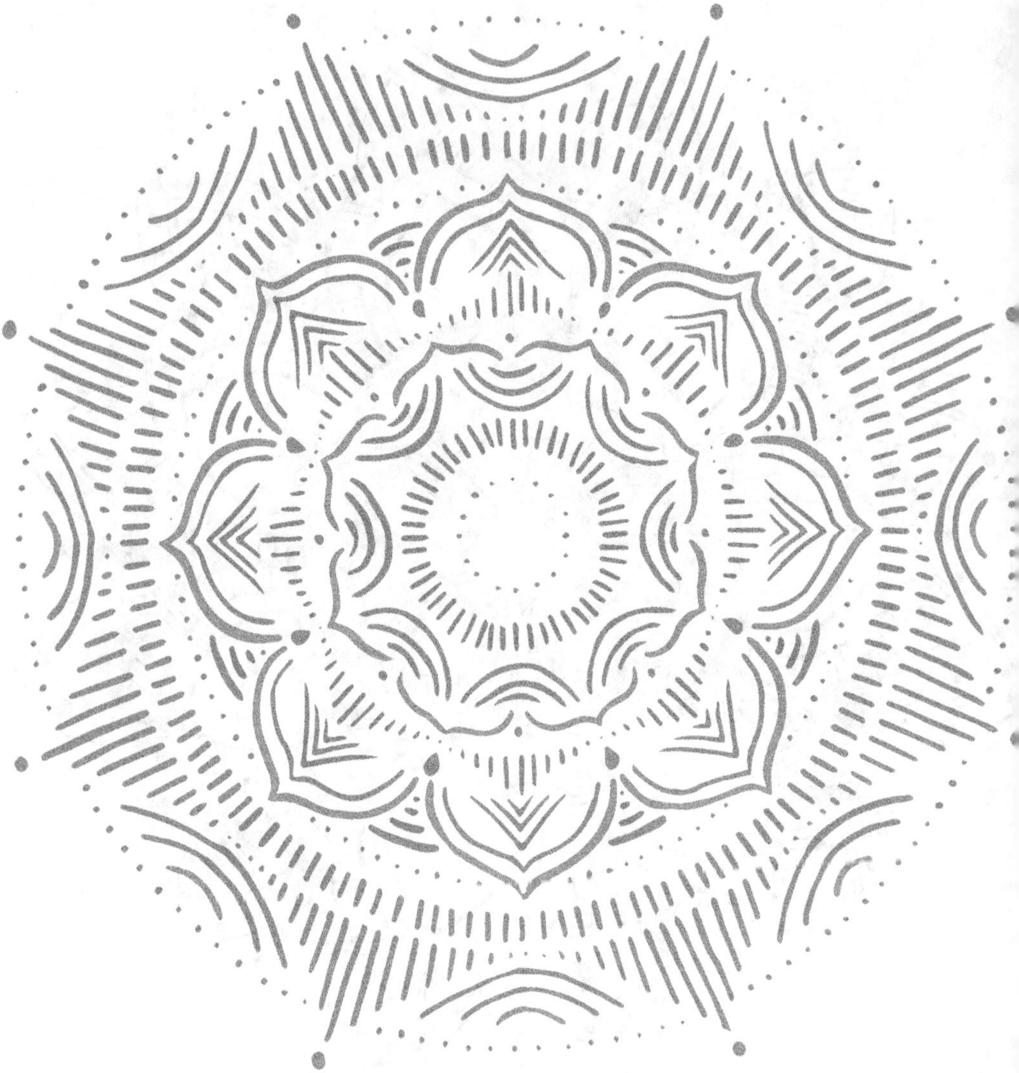

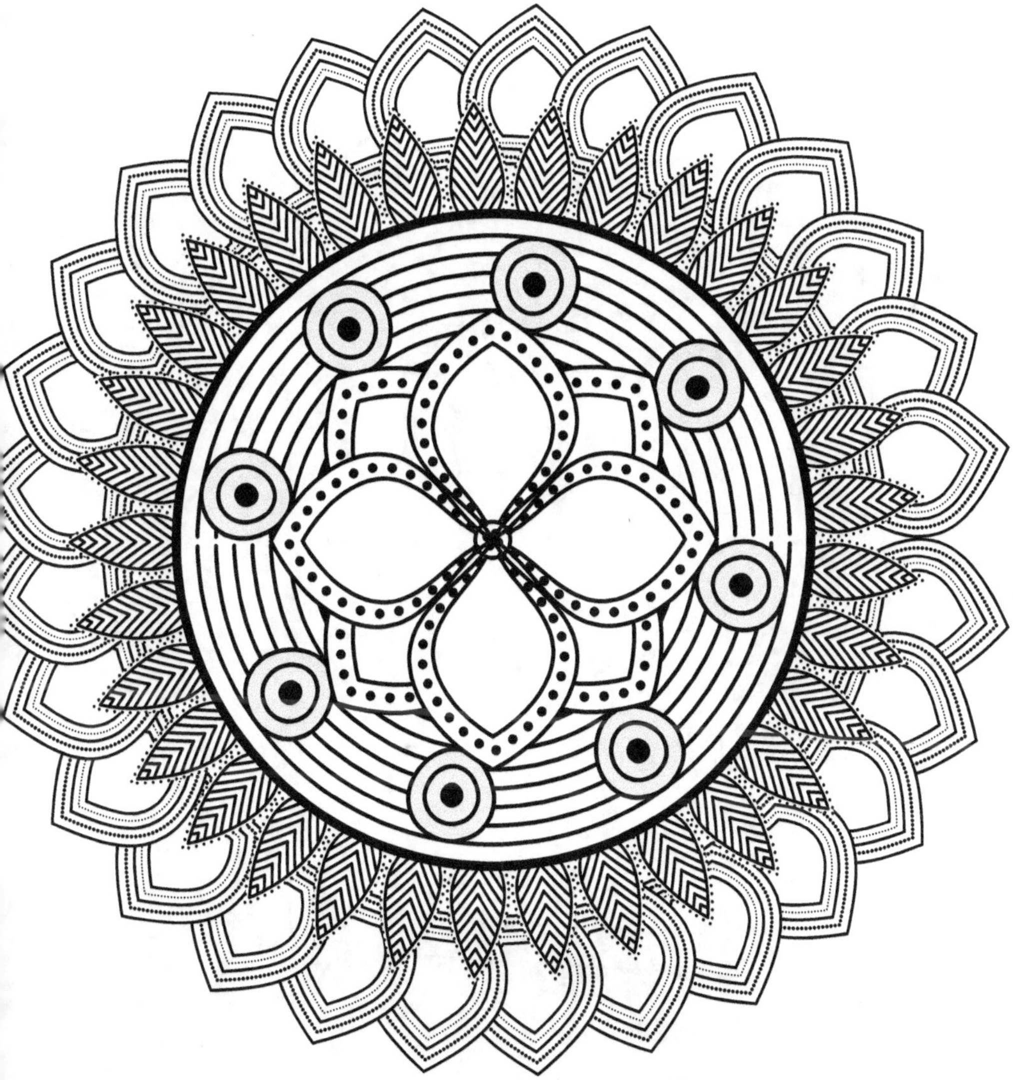

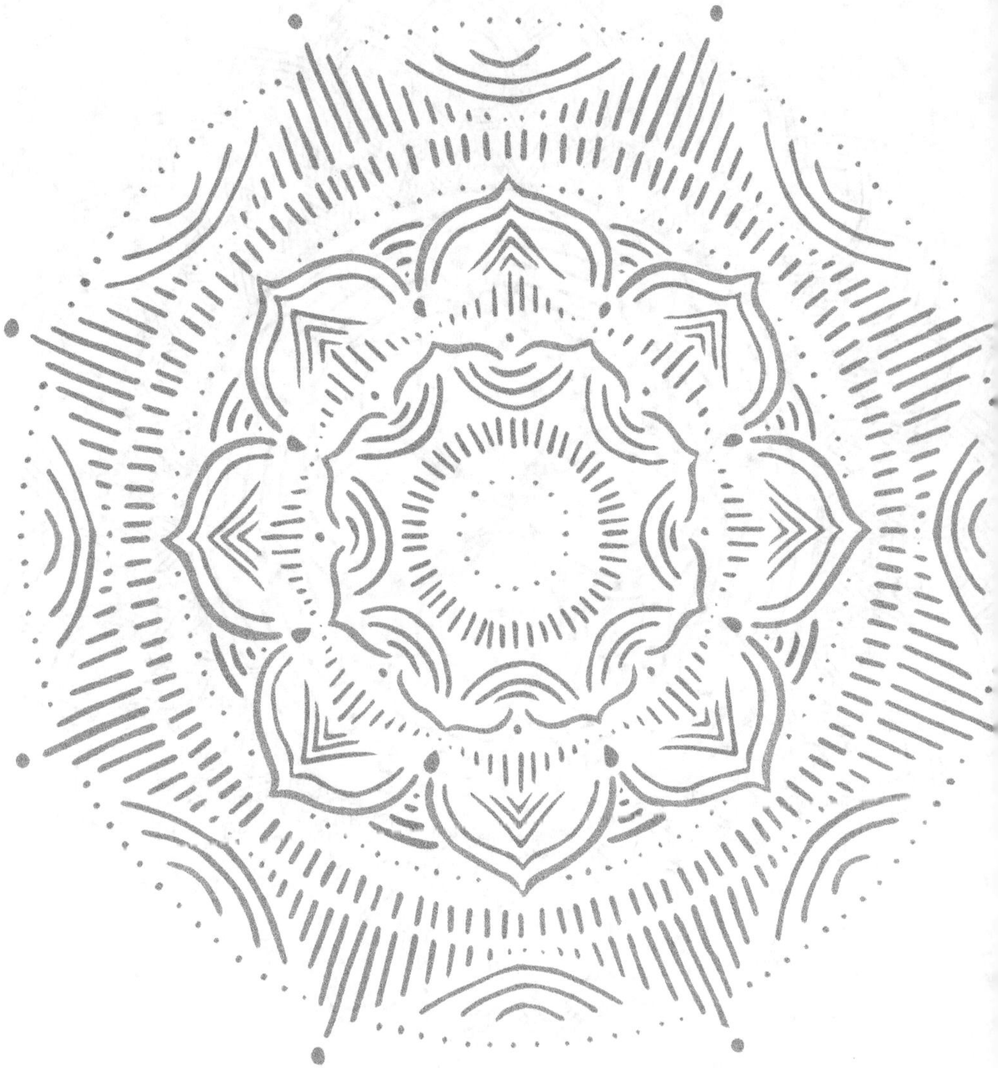

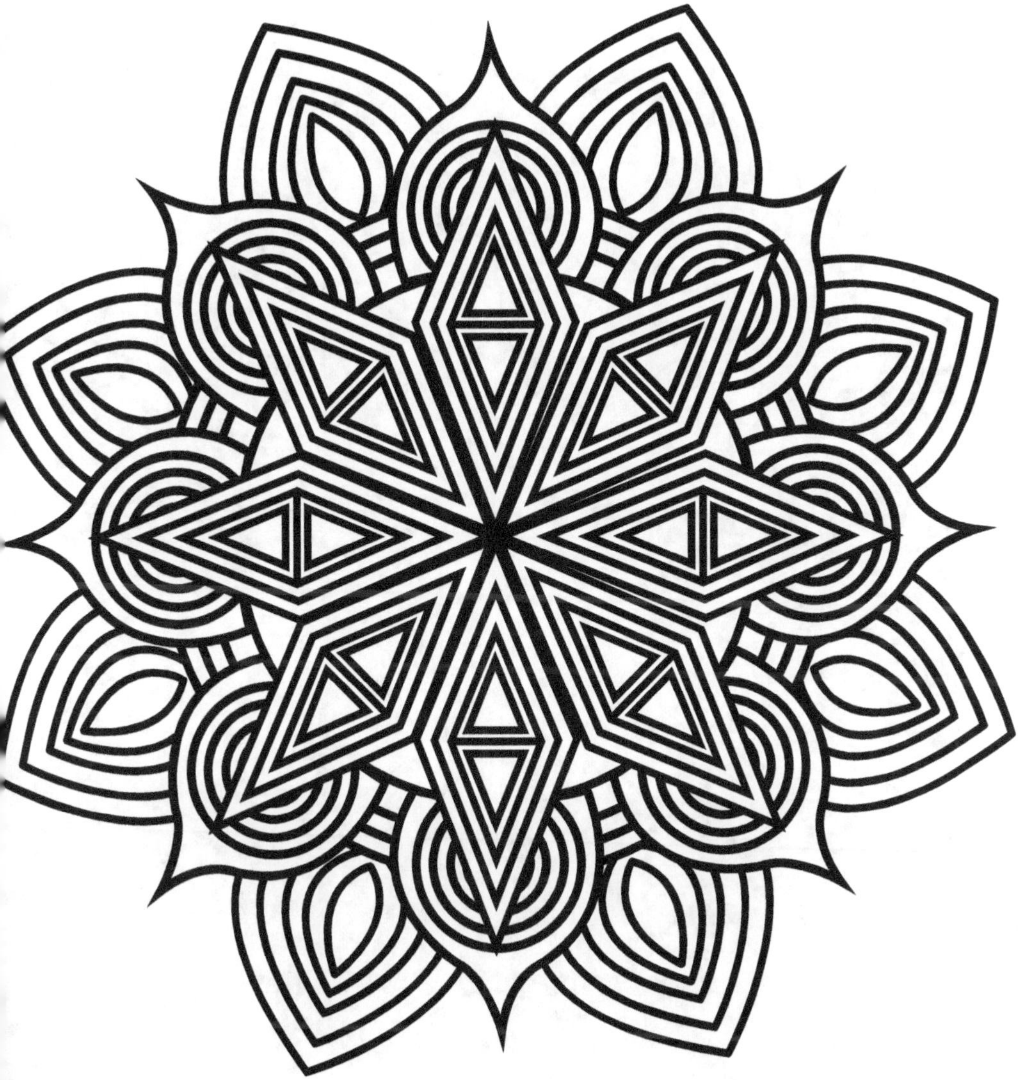

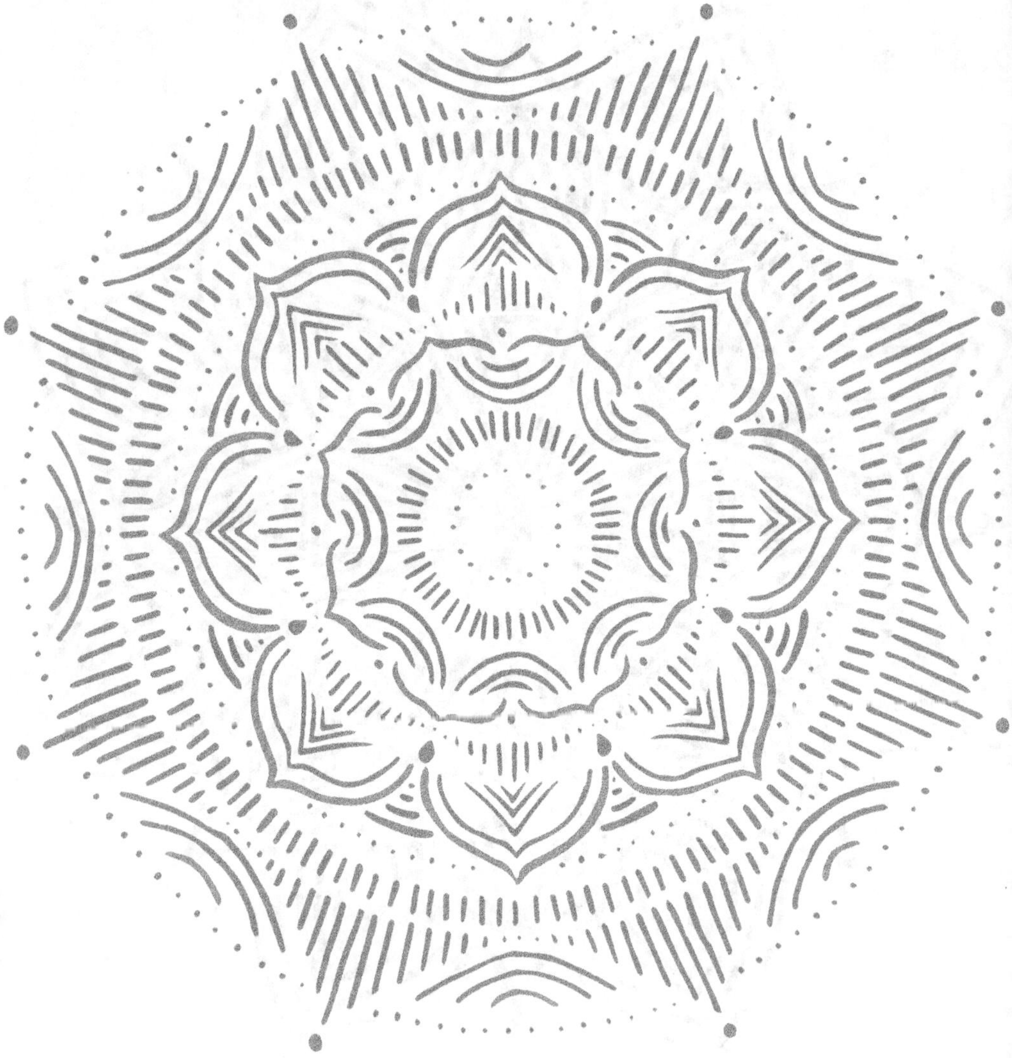

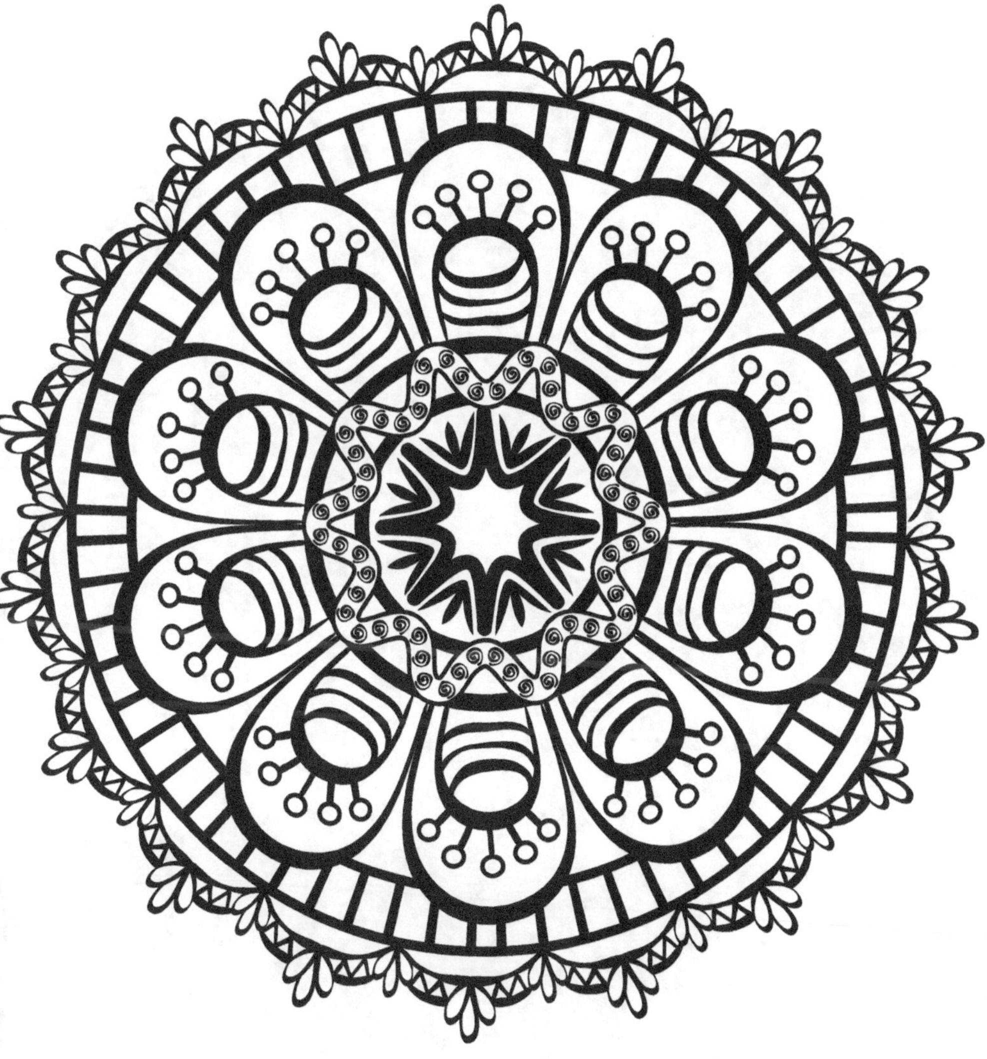

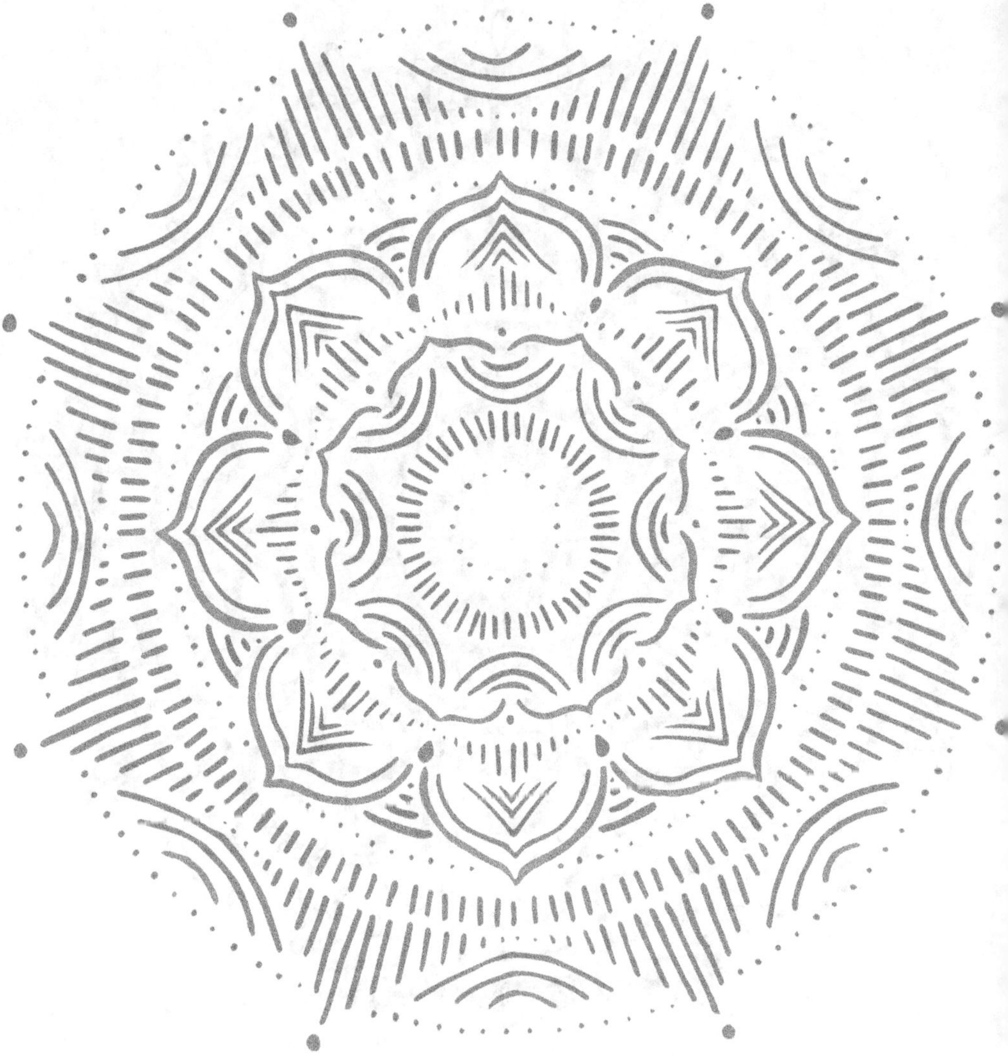

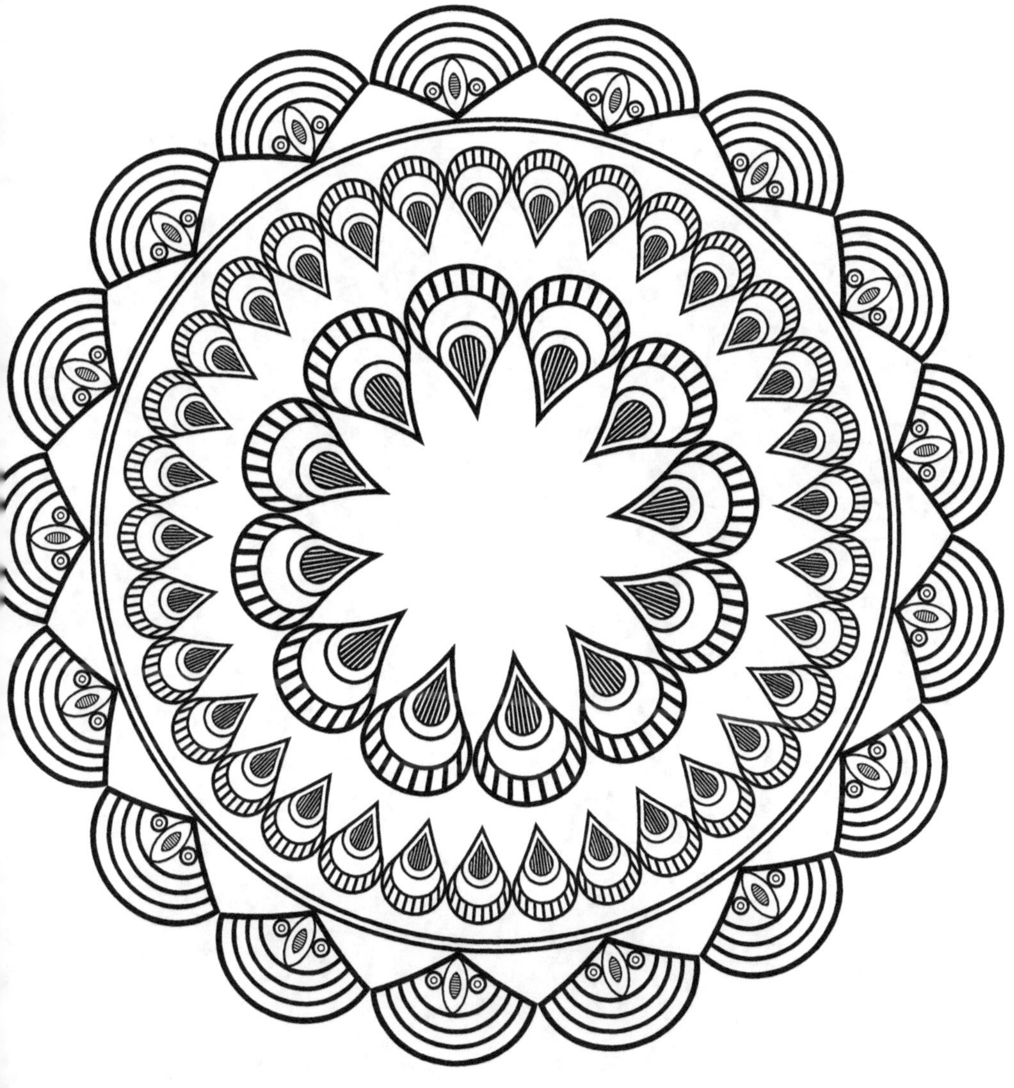

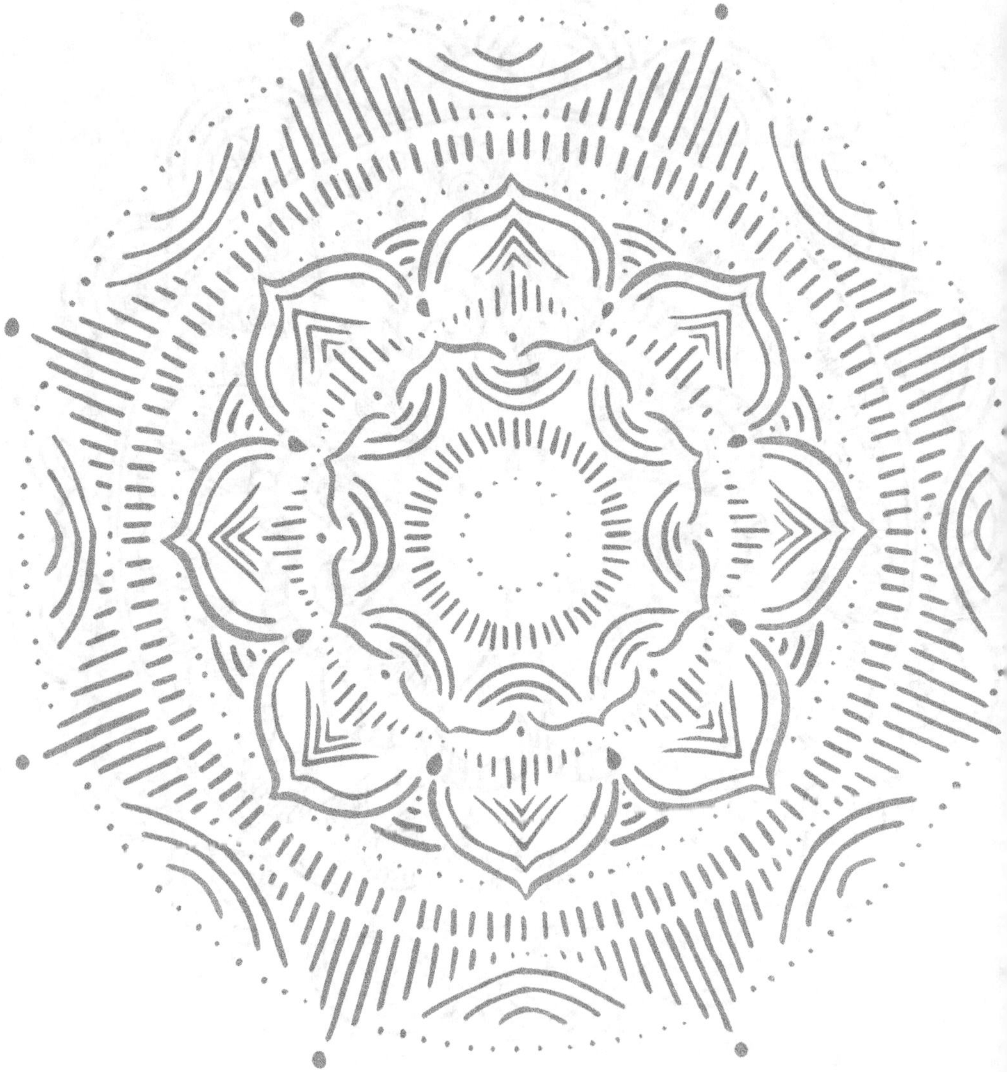

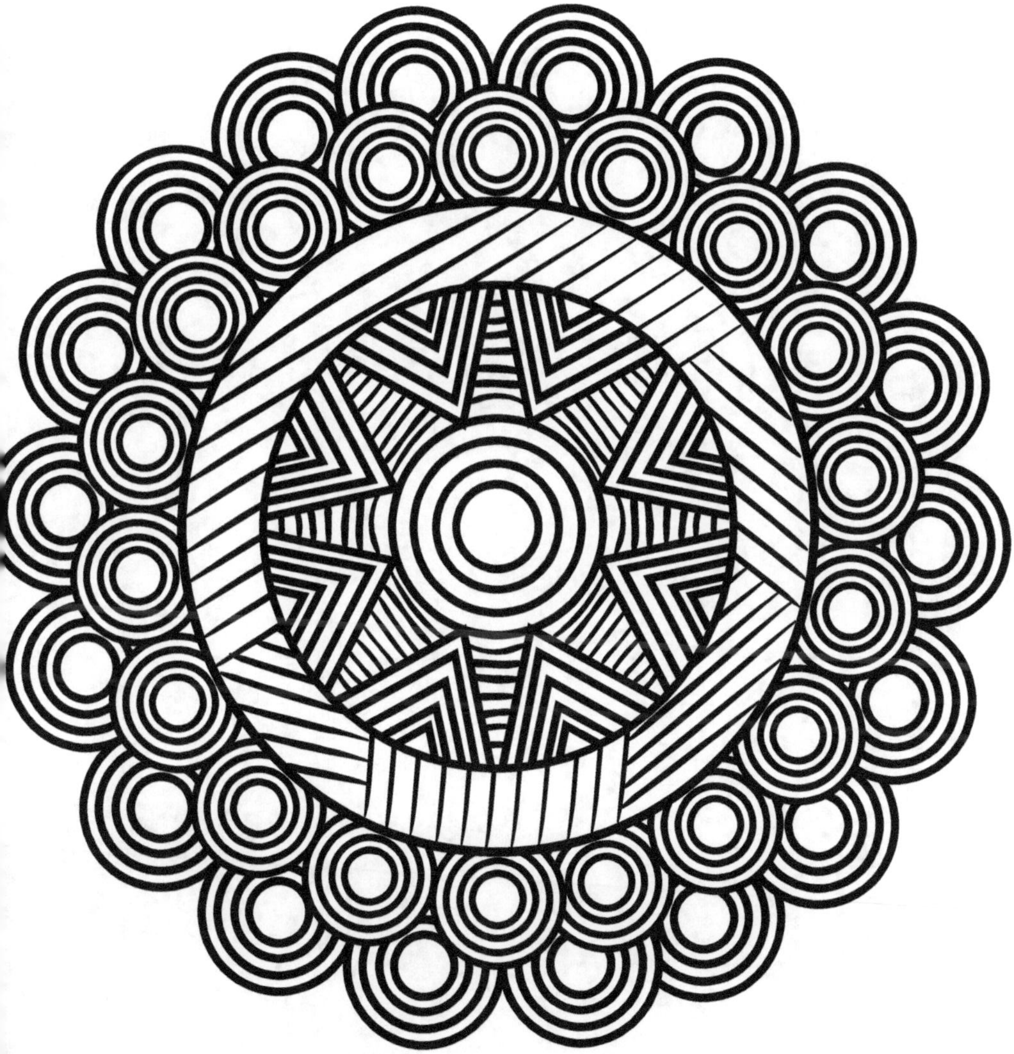

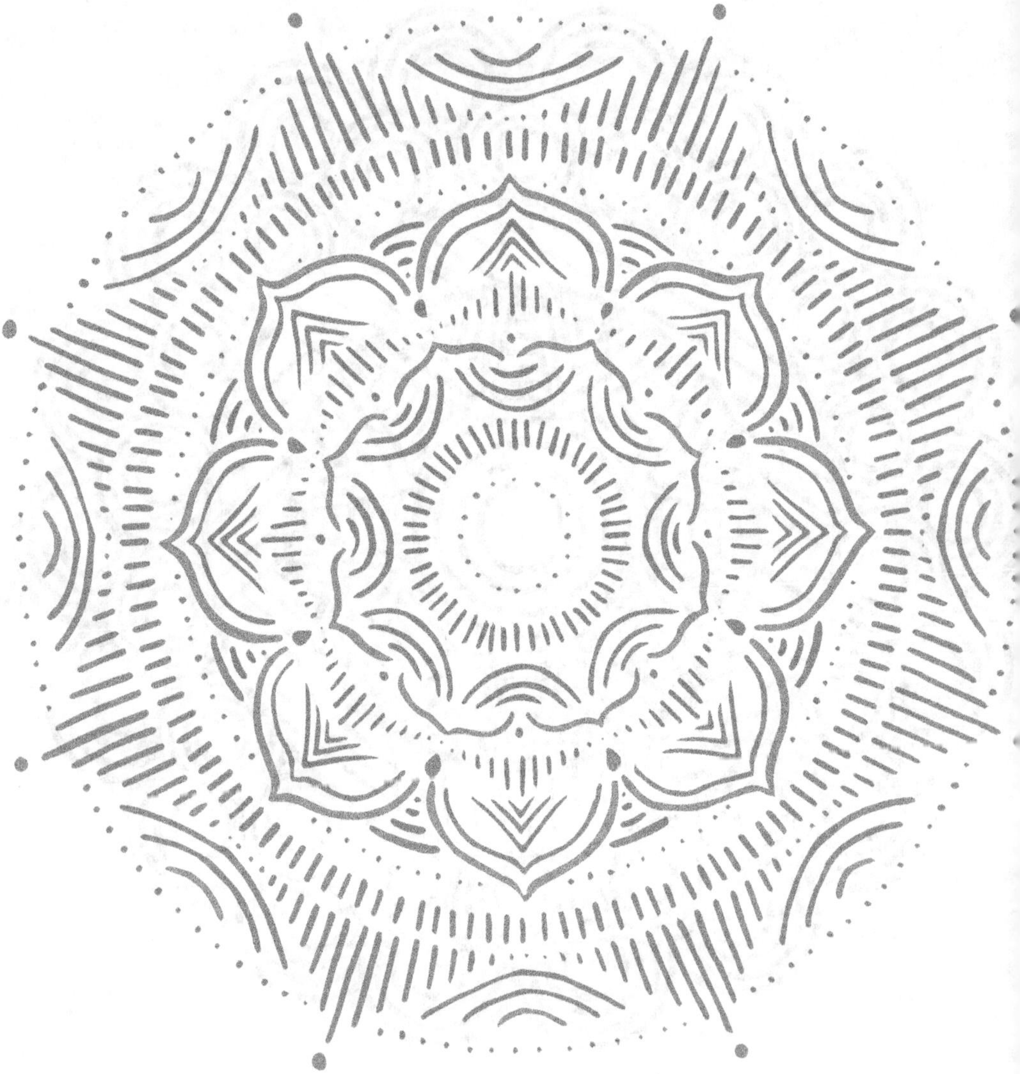

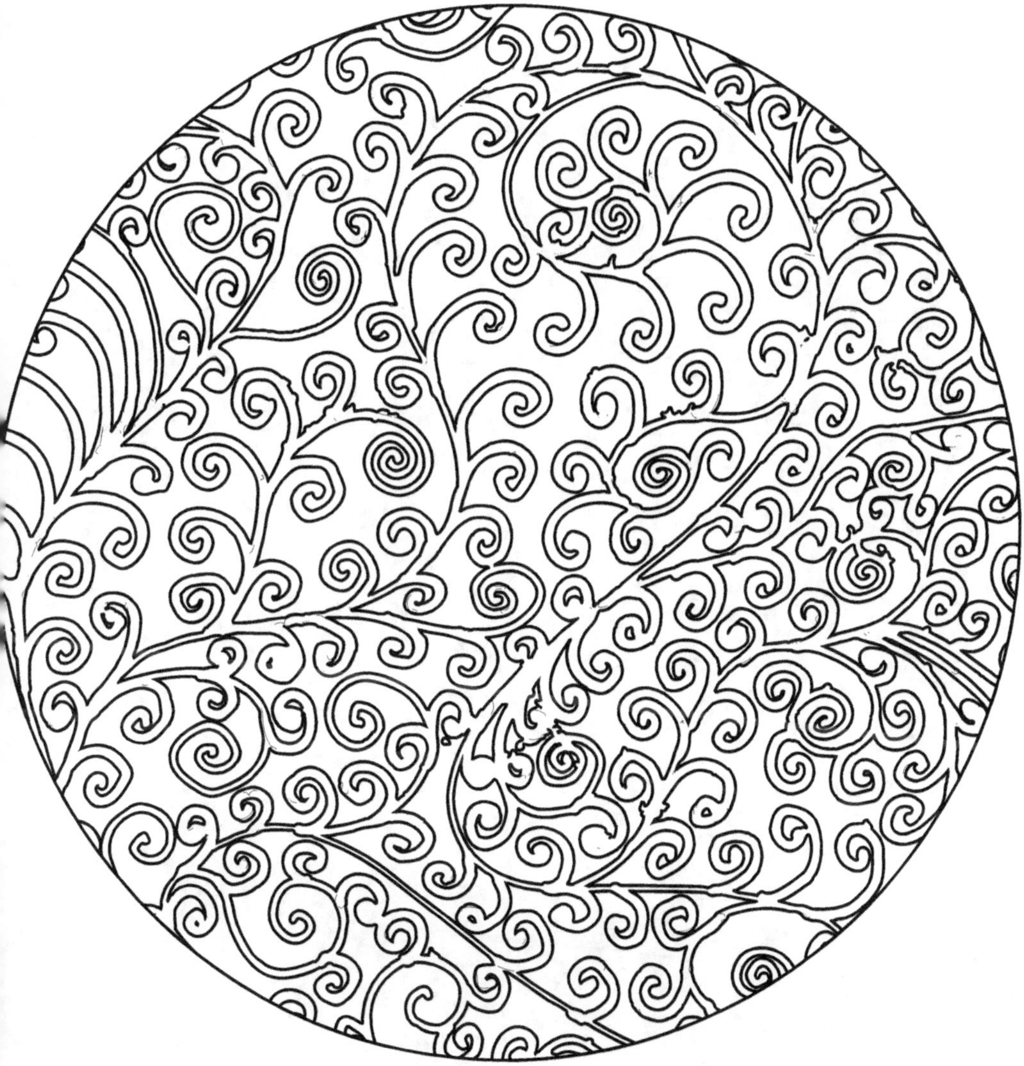

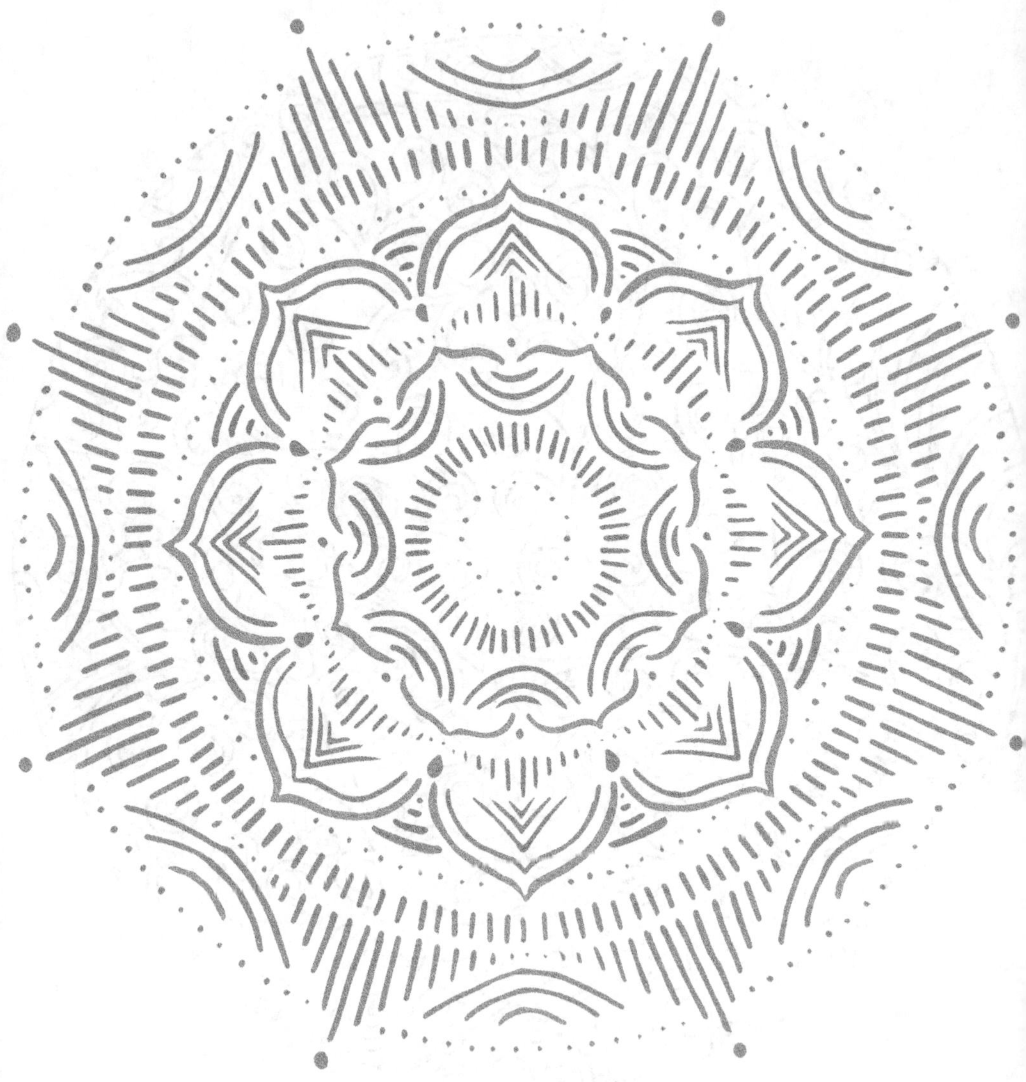

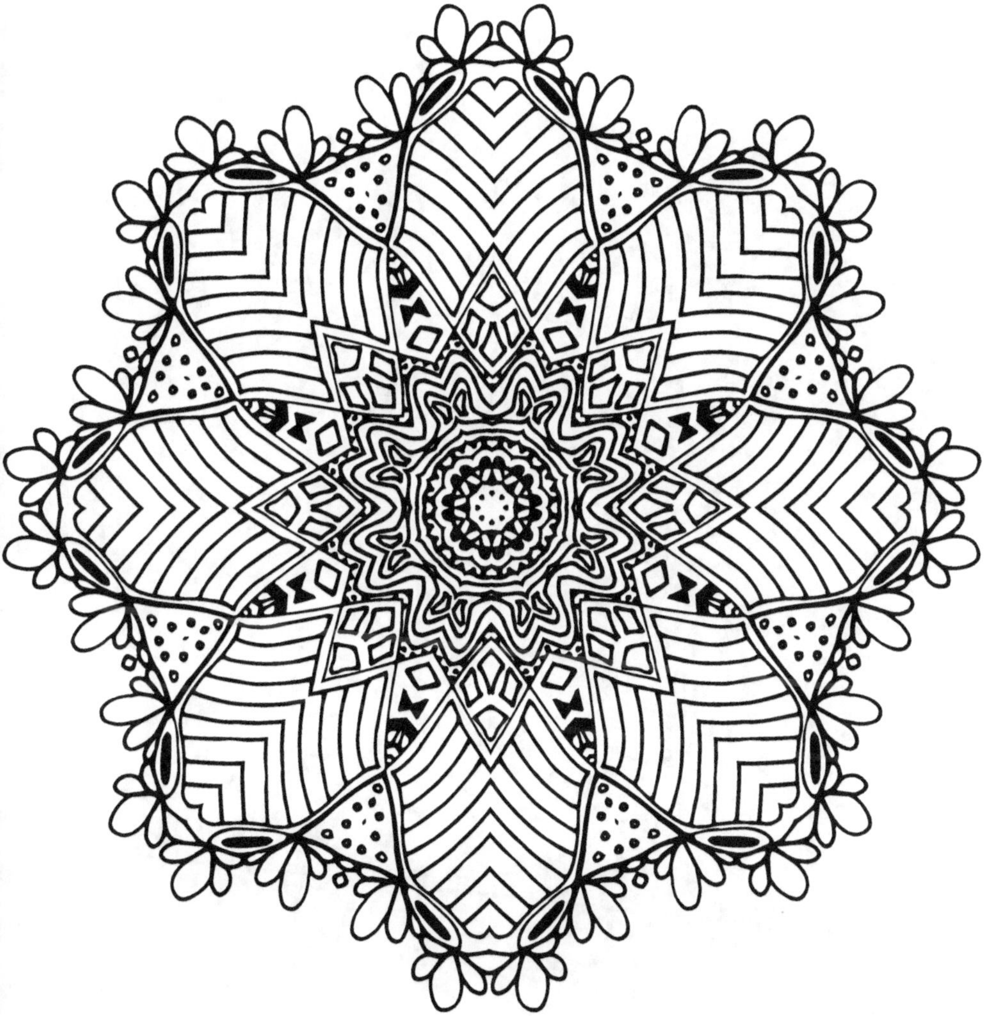

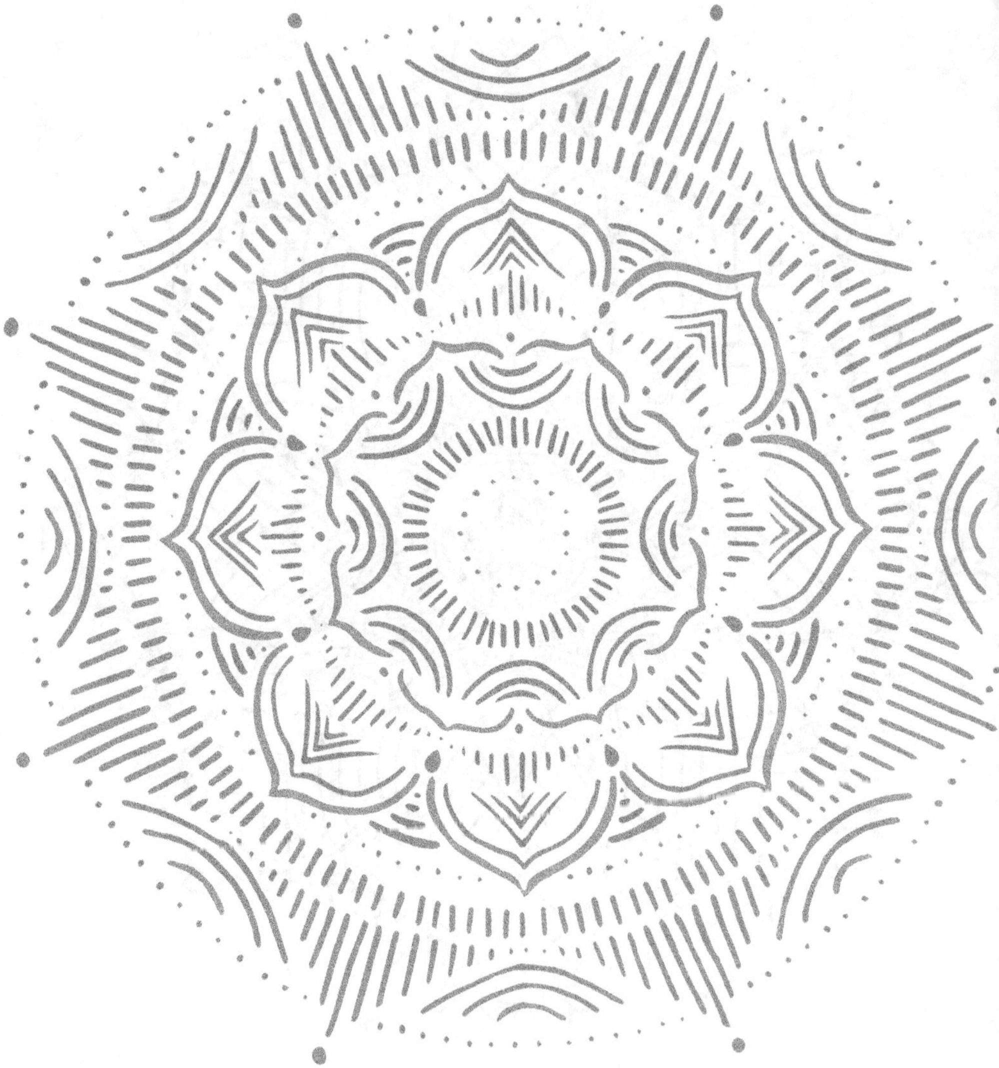

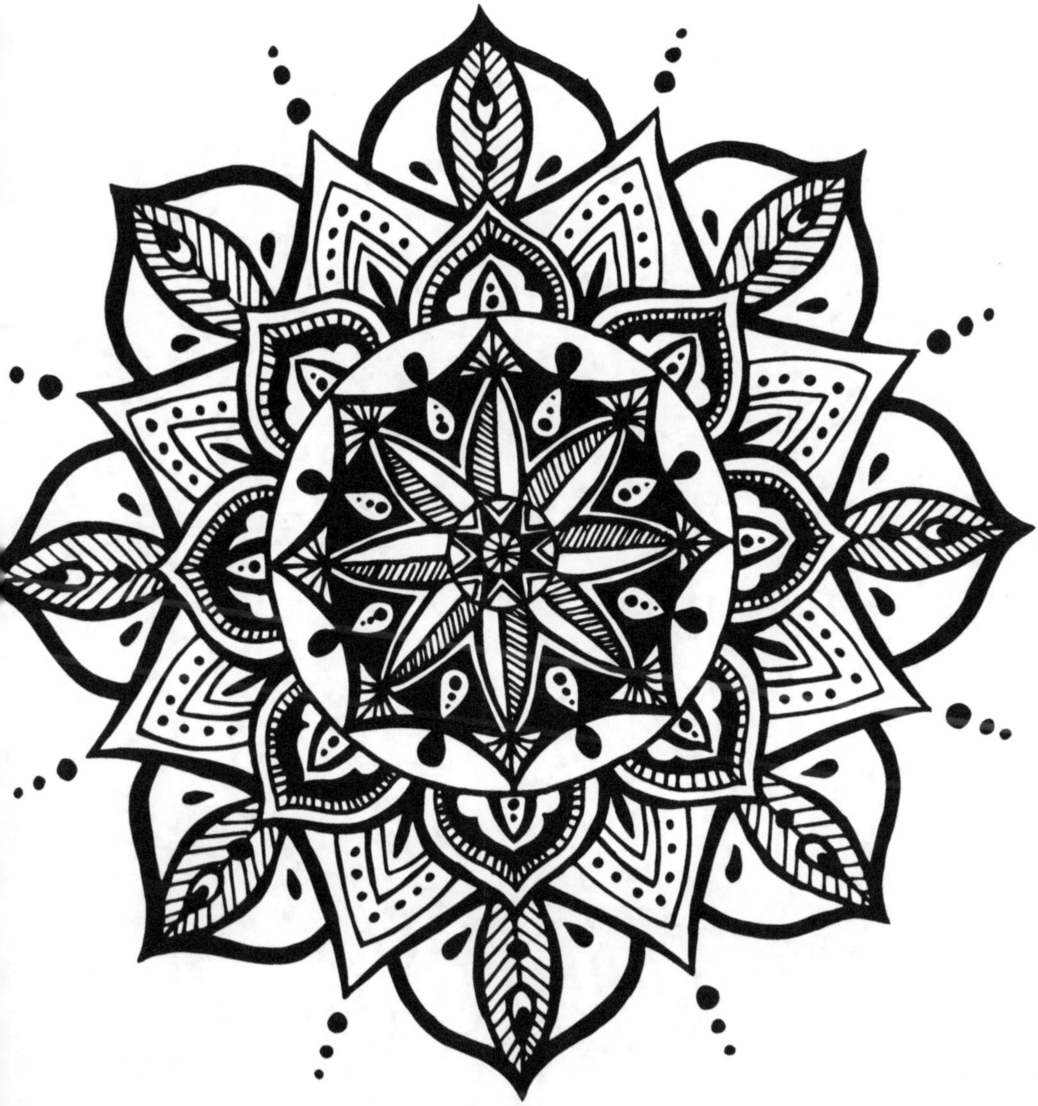

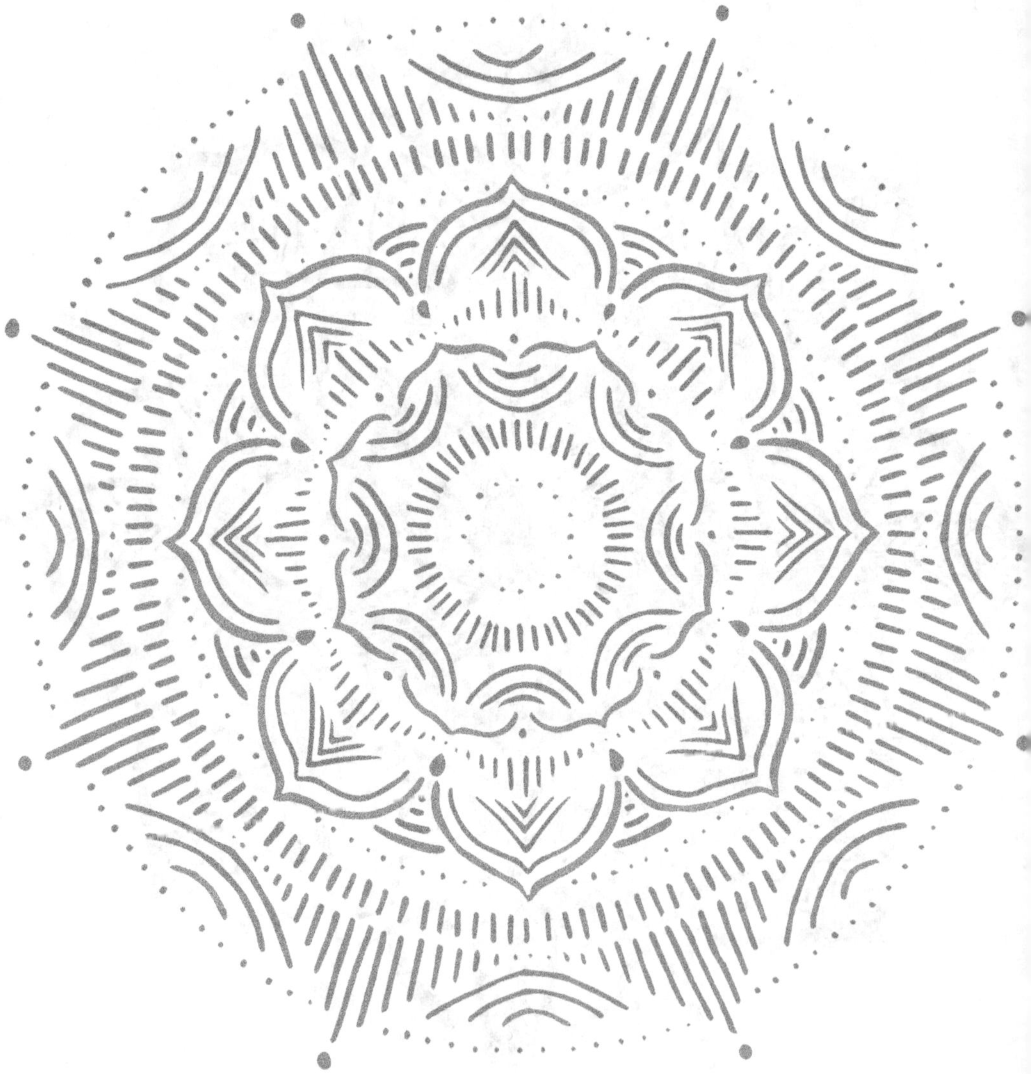

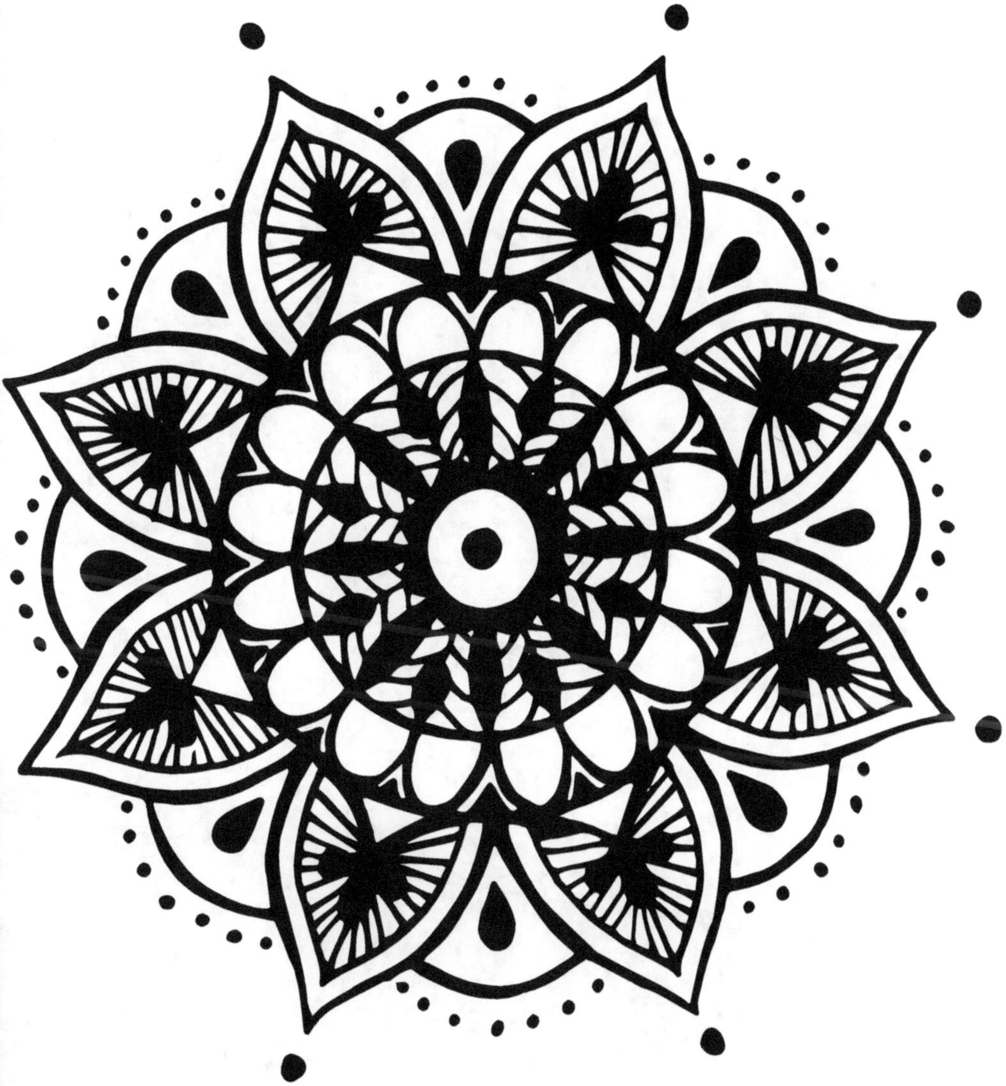

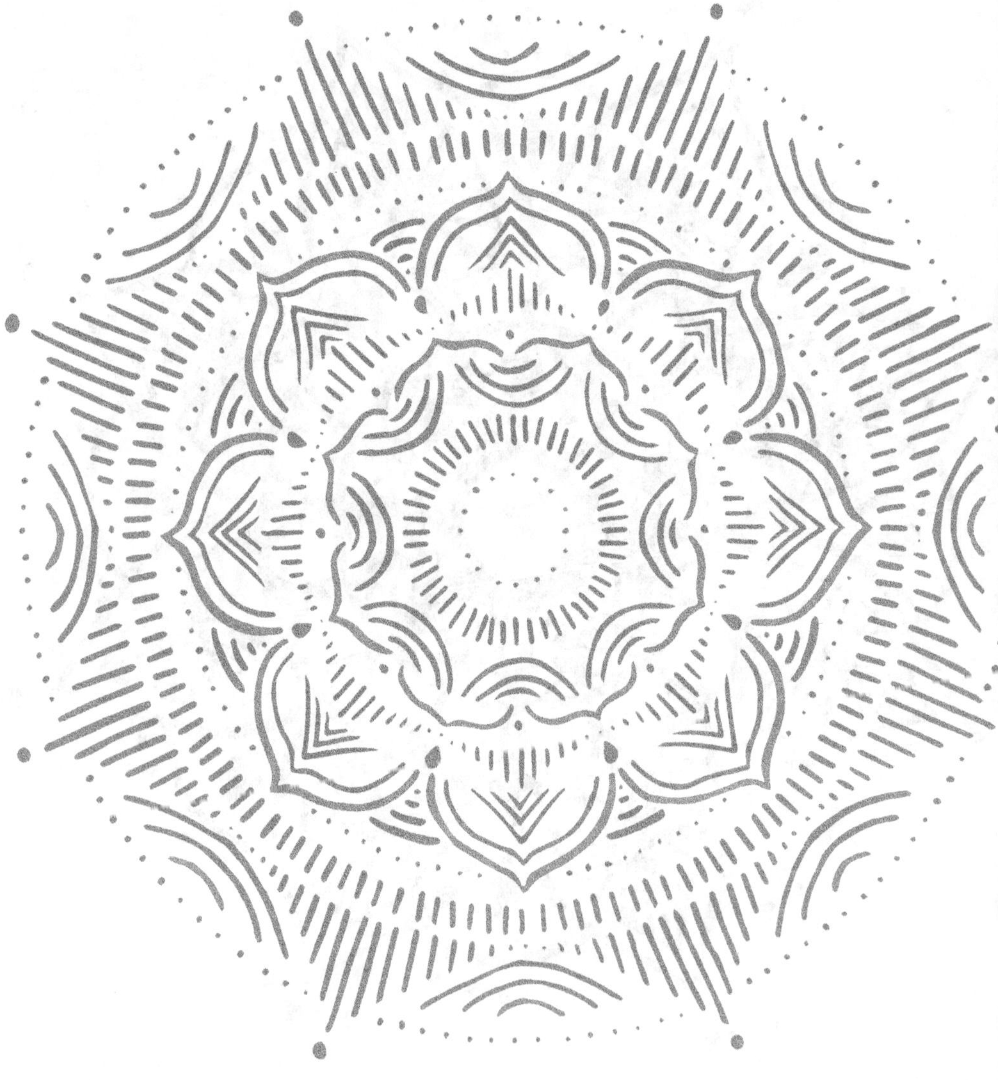

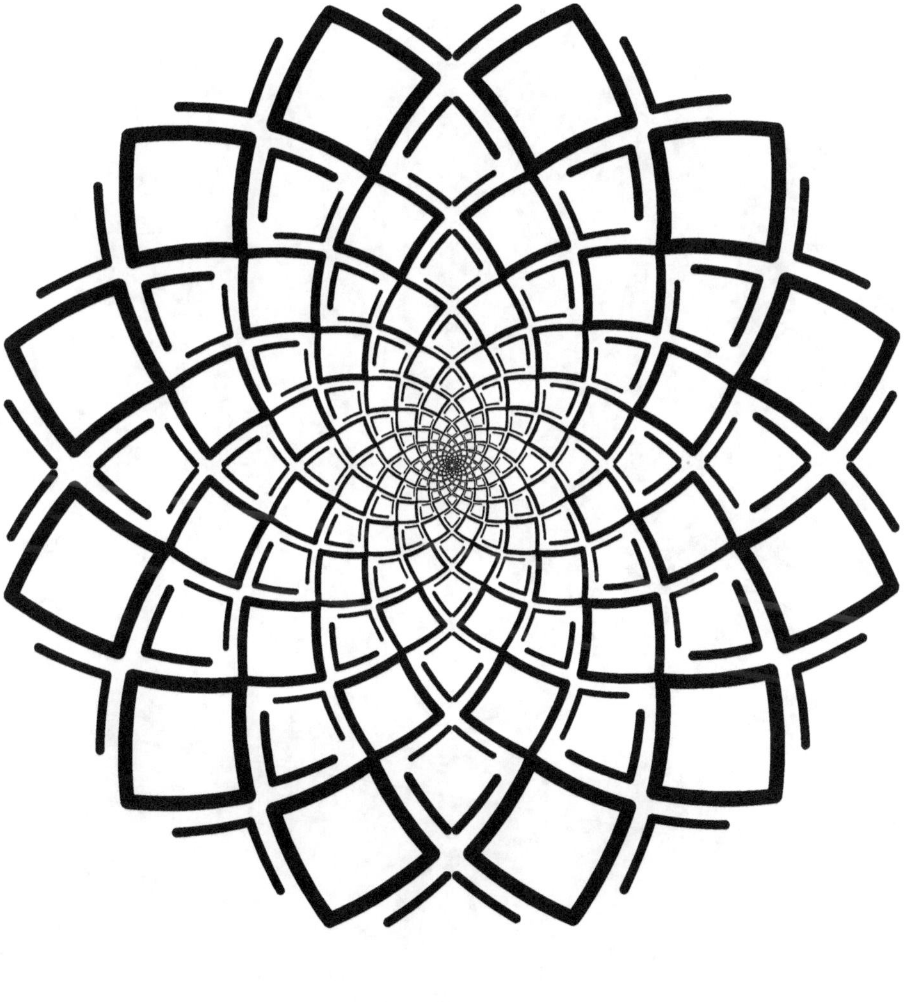

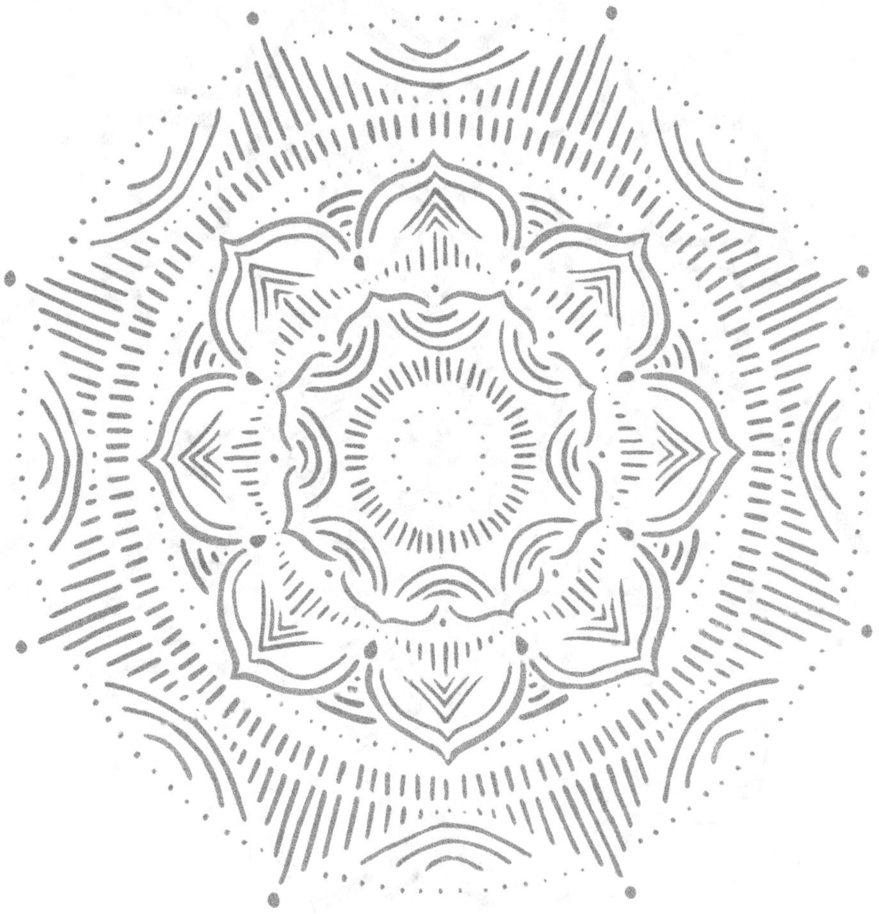

www.ingramcontent.com/pod-product-compliance
Lightning Source LLC
Chambersburg PA
CBHW070826220526
45466CB00002B/764
9798580519579